The Apprenticeship That Saved My Life

PRAISE FOR
THE APPRENTICESHIP THAT SAVED MY LIFE

Cory McCray has drawn on his life's experiences to forge a compelling story of redemption and reinvention. It is both a guidebook and a guidepost for many in today's generation of young people, their parents and school advisers. Most of all it's a real testimony to the power of using apprenticeships to beat the odds, proving that it is not how you start in life that counts … it's how you finish.

Kweisi Mfume, author of *No Free Ride: From the Mean Streets to the Mainstream*

Cory McCray's story is one of resilience and redemption. An apprenticeship transformed his life. His inspirational story highlights that apprenticeships are not just career pathways—they are engines of economic empowerment. His leadership underscores the importance of investing in workforce development to create lasting opportunities for working families and future generations.

Tom Perez, former U.S. secretary of labor

Cory McCray's journey is a testament to the power of opportunity, perseverance, and community investment. His story reflects the very essence of what it means to create pathways to success for hardworking Marylanders. *The Apprenticeship That Saved My Life* is more than a book—it's a blueprint for empowering the next generation with the skills and resources to achieve economic mobility.

Angela D. Alsobrooks, groundbreaking Maryland leader and former Prince George's County executive

Cory McCray takes us on a journey of his life and work through compelling and personal storytelling. He illuminates a path forward for young people in every ZIP code—showing that through hard work, a skilled apprenticeship and a union card, the pathway to the middle class is within reach. But he does more than provide a "cheat sheet" on job training. He does what his mother did for him—offering a loving hand and reminding young people that they are not alone. His leadership shows how investing in skills, access, and economic mobility builds power for working people and strengthens our communities.

Elizabeth H. Shuler, president, AFL-CIO

Cory's journey is proof that when we invest in people, we invest in the future. His leadership shows that apprenticeships are more than just jobs—they are pathways to equity, stability, and generational change.

Michael Tubbs, author of *The Deeper the Roots* and former mayor of Stockton, California

Cory McCray's story is a testament to the power of apprenticeships in transforming lives and opening doors to opportunity. His journey—from apprentice to legislator—serves as an inspiring road map for students, educators, and policymakers alike. *The Apprenticeship That Saved My Life* is a must-read for anyone seeking to bridge the gap between education and economic mobility.

Cassie Motz, executive director, CollegeBound Foundation

For decades, the United States, unfortunately, elevated college and university as the top and primary path to the American dream. However, over the past ten years, with greater public and private sector investment, more opportunities, and success stories like Cory's to highlight how extraordinary apprenticeship is at providing people with skills, meaningful work, mentorship, and opportunity, we have been able to expand access to that dream. We still have a long way to go to introduce more people to this effective pathway and this book will play an important role in that amplification. Cory's journey is deeply inspiring and his willingness to turn it into a playbook for others to easily follow is a profound gift for all!

Suzi LeVine, former U.S. ambassador to Switzerland and Liechtenstein

The Apprenticeship That Saved My Life is a powerful reminder of what's possible when young people have real access to meaningful career-connected opportunities. Cory McCray's story underscores the importance of meeting individuals where they are and equipping them with the tools to build not just careers, but lasting economic stability. It is both an inspiration and a call to action for everyone working to expand equitable access to education and workforce opportunities—particularly through apprenticeship.

Chas Ackley, executive director, Urban Alliance

You don't need to be a Baltimorean to love and learn from *The Apprenticeship That Saved My Life*. If you are a student figuring out your path, a parent trying to navigate with your child, or a guidance counselor steering through rapidly changing terrain, *The Apprenticeship That Saved My Life* will be a game-changer for all.

Angelique Power, chief executive officer, The Skillman Foundation

THE APPRENTICESHIP THAT SAVED MY LIFE

A GUIDEBOOK TO NAVIGATING EARN-WHILE-YOU-LEARN
OPPORTUNITIES OF A LIFETIME

CORY V. McCRAY
FOREWORD BY BRANDON SCOTT

NEW YORK

LONDON • NASHVILLE • MELBOURNE • VANCOUVER

THE APPRENTICESHIP THAT SAVED MY LIFE
A Guidebook to Navigating Earn-While-You-Learn Opportunities of a Lifetime

© 2025 Cory V. McCray

All rights reserved. No portion of this book may be reproduced, stored in a retrieval system, or transmitted in any form or by any means—electronic, mechanical, photocopy, recording, scanning, or other—except for brief quotations in critical reviews or articles, without the prior written permission of the publisher.

Published in New York, New York, by Morgan James Publishing. Morgan James is a trademark of Morgan James, LLC. www.MorganJamesPublishing.com

Proudly distributed by Publishers Group West®

A **FREE** ebook edition is available for you or a friend with the purchase of this print book.

CLEARLY SIGN YOUR NAME ABOVE

Instructions to claim your free ebook edition:
1. Visit MorganJamesBOGO.com
2. Sign your name CLEARLY in the space above
3. Complete the form and submit a photo of this entire page
4. You or your friend can download the ebook to your preferred device

ISBN 9781636986890 paperback
ISBN 9781636986906 ebook
Library of Congress Control Number: 2025931805

Cover Design by:
Matt Kayser
Creative Print Group

Interior Design by:
Chris Treccani
www.3dogcreative.net

Morgan James is a proud partner of Habitat for Humanity Peninsula and Greater Williamsburg. Partners in building since 2006.

Get involved today! Visit: www.morgan-james-publishing.com/giving-back

DEDICATION

To my mother, who never gave up on her son; to my wife, Demetria, who has stood by me through my worst and my best; and to my children, Kennedy, Reagan, CJ and Bryson, may you find within yourselves the tools to achieve dreams beyond your imagination.

TABLE OF CONTENTS

Foreword . . . . *xv*
Introduction . . . . *xix*

Chapter 1:   A Hard Introduction to Apprenticeships 1
Chapter 2:   Earn While You Learn 19
Chapter 3:   Preparing for Apprenticeships
             While in High School 33
Chapter 4:   How Can an Apprenticeship Be Free?. . 49
Chapter 5:   Building Better Study Habits
             and Surviving the Apprenticeship. 61
Chapter 6:   Gaining Mentorship Through
             Apprenticeships 73
Chapter 7:   Working with Difficult People and
             Navigating Difficult Situations in an
             Apprenticeship. 85
Chapter 8:   Pre-Apprenticeships Versus
             Apprenticeships 99
Chapter 9:   Understanding the Different
             Trade Apprenticeships 113

Chapter 10: Apprentice to Entrepreneur 129
Chapter 11: Additional Resources 141

Acknowledgments *145*
About the Author *149*

FOREWORD

In the spring of 2010, during my final months as a mayoral staffer before launching my first campaign for Baltimore City Council, I attended a community event in Belair-Edison—something I had done dozens of times before. But fate had decided this one would be different.

As he often did, Tony Dawson, then-president of the community association, pulled me aside and said he wanted me to meet someone. "As two young Black men doing work in the community, you should know each other," he told me. We walked down the 3500 block of Parklawn Avenue, where he introduced me to a young electrician named Cory McCray. Like me, Cory was from "over west," though we both now lived in Northeast Baltimore. I still remember Tony's words that day: "Cory is an electrician, but, Brandon, I really think you young guys are the future leaders of our community."

That day, Cory and I exchanged numbers, unaware that our futures—and the future of our city—would be forever changed by that chance meeting.

In the months and years that followed, Cory and I realized just how much we had in common. Like so many young

Black men who grew up in Baltimore during our time, we shared the experiences of living in neighborhoods impacted by violence, navigating a world with limited opportunities, and coming of age during the era of zero-tolerance policing. But beyond that, we shared a deep, unwavering desire for a better future—not just for ourselves and our families, but for our entire community.

Early in our friendship, as Cory prepared to run for office for the first time, I gave him my coveted community leaders directory. I knew it was risky. Suddenly, another young man, not from East Baltimore, had access to every leader's phone number and knew when every meeting happened. I knew it would ruffle feathers in the political establishment. But I also knew it was the right thing to do. I had to pay it forward, no matter the consequences. And I was right.

Today, no one can imagine East Baltimore without Senator Cory McCray. But at that time, Delegate McCray was far from a guarantee. I often wonder how different my life—and the future of our city—would be if we had never met, if we had never built a friendship, or if I had never taken that chance to support another young Black man determined to make a difference.

This book is a powerful, unfiltered look into the life of a man who has lived and experienced more in his lifetime than most would in nine lives. It is a bold, deeply personal narrative that does not shy away from past mistakes or shortcomings. Instead, it confronts them head-on, something many cannot do because most have never lived those experiences.

What makes this book so impactful is not just the raw storytelling, but the lessons woven throughout. Cory shares how he transformed from a young man carrying guns and leading in the wrong direction to a master electrician, a business owner, and, ultimately, a public servant—all through the undeniable power of a mother's love and his own determination. But this book does more than tell a story. It serves as a blueprint, a guide for anyone who finds themselves in a similar situation, showing them that transformation is possible.

In fact, this work could, and probably should, be required reading for young people seeking a second chance. In his own eloquent way, Cory is paying it forward, speaking directly to those who, like he once did, may feel lost or without hope.

To those who read this book: I hope you recognize it for what it is—a love letter to the forgotten, the overlooked, and the underestimated. And in doing so, I hope you come to understand the incredible journey of a young man who once found himself behind walls, only to rise as one of the greatest public servants, husbands, and fathers I have ever known.

Brandon Scott, February 2025

INTRODUCTION

I grew up in Baltimore City neighborhoods filled with often-crushing challenges, in ZIP codes that I now realize are built to fail.

One day, when I was around twelve, our community was rocked by news that the guy who sold Christmas trees in the Belvedere Garden Shopping Center parking lot had been robbed and shot at.

Police pressured the neighborhood over the next few weeks as they sought clues about who was responsible.

The culprit: a childhood friend who we'll call Phil.

Phil was three years older than me. We hung out with homeboys in different circles but would all congregate on our block at the regular spot by the apartments he lived in. We smoked marijuana, played pickup basketball and football, fought with kids from rival neighborhoods, and filled our idle time with mischief.

Phil was arrested and locked up for more than twenty months. He came back to the same neighborhood—a place with limited choices and opportunities—and used his skills to grow from a low-level drug dealer of marijuana and crack cocaine to a mid-level operative moving pounds of product.

Fast-forward a decade.

I had just completed an apprenticeship program run by the International Brotherhood of Electrical Workers, earning good money as a journeyman while investing in houses in Baltimore that produced rental income.

Family and friends were proud that I was beating the streets and overcoming the odds of jail and death. I had become a leader in my small universe, and, ready or not, a role model.

One day, my phone rang. It was Phil. He heard my story and was seeking a lifeline.

He told me about just coming home from another short incarceration. Desperation filled his throat as he talked about wanting a different route, both for him and his daughter.

Phil knew that I was no smarter than he was, and maybe not even a harder worker. I just caught a break and took advantage of it. Could he duplicate that route?

At that point, I wasn't entirely convinced I could stay on the path I was on. Did I have the energy? Would I slip back and be consumed by the neighborhoods that offered no way out for too many? I was still learning my own strengths and weaknesses. But Phil needed a hand.

People don't realize that there are small windows of opportunity when a person reaches a life juncture and is willing to share vulnerabilities and accept change. Those windows may open only briefly, so if you are a parent, guidance counselor, or mentor—you must act quickly before the windows close, forced shut by the daily demands of bills or the allure of a well-trodden lifestyle.

I had no choice. I accepted the responsibility. I'd help Phil out.

We agreed to meet at the IBEW apprenticeship program office, and Phil filled out the application forms. I hadn't realized that he had not graduated from high school, which meant that he wasn't currently eligible for the program.

But he was enrolled in a General Educational Development (GED) program, trying to get across the finish line to a diploma. Soon enough, Phil was offered a job as an apprentice's helper on a large hospital jobsite in downtown Baltimore as he navigated the requirements of the apprenticeship application.

I would receive reports that Phil was a hard worker and was doing well. I wasn't surprised. I know from personal experience that if you have the skills to avoid robbers, police, and the jealousy of peers in neighborhoods like East Baltimore, then you have more than enough discipline to put in eight hours of hard work on a construction site.

This opportunity would keep Phil off the corners of Baltimore City and, for up to ten hours out of the day, in a constructive learning environment, acquiring on-the-job training and growth opportunities.

Phil would earn his GED, meet all other requirements and even collect letters of recommendation from the journeymen who worked with him on jobsites. He was on his way.

Phil's story has always stuck with me. It was the first time I realized that the choices I had made that put my life on a path to success could serve as a road map for others.

It made me realize that I needed to embrace being a role model, and that it was both an honor and a responsibility to lend a hand to others.

And that is why I am now sharing that knowledge in this book. One-on-one mentoring and guidance are powerful, but I want to scale them up, and make a broader impact in the lives of young people in our communities.

My life was saved by an apprenticeship. I know that others can be saved. This book will help.

About This Book

The Apprenticeship That Saved My Life is my intentional disruption of a failing system, informed by twenty years of captured knowledge.

The tools I applied and failures and successes I endured can serve as a resource to help others reach their full potential and break cycles. Over years, I have realized that, especially for young people, "we don't know what we don't know." But in this book, there is knowledge. I know it, because I've earned it.

I share not just my story but the collective narrative of my family and community, aiming to break a generational cycle of poverty and lack of financial literacy. My story is, I believe, a testament to the power of perseverance, mentorship, and seizing opportunities—a cheat code I'm determined to share for overcoming arbitrary barriers for our children and future generations.

Readers will follow my journey from a troubled youth expelled from several Baltimore City schools through a series of encounters with Maryland's juvenile and adult facilities due to firearms and drug-related issues.

I faced adult charges twice before I turned eighteen, but with the help of my mother, who you will meet later, I eventually transformed my life, becoming an IBEW electrician and a thriving entrepreneur with a real estate portfolio covering more than a half-dozen properties by age twenty-five.

Eventually, I was elected to the Maryland State Senate representing the community I grew up in, and focused on policy solutions to ensure that our young minds reach their highest potential.

At every step of the way, I gained knowledge that I wish I had learned earlier. That's why I'm writing it down now.

Each chapter in this book has the potential to unleash powerful navigation tools, regardless of socioeconomic status.

Readers will see why learning a trade is a viable alternative for those seeking options outside a college or university education, which often burdens students with suffocating debt.

We will examine how to find apprenticeship programs and how to prepare for and apply them. We will also have a hard but important discussion about what students need to get from K-12 educational institutions, even as these schools don't prepare young minds with the tools to familiarize themselves with these valuable opportunities.

We examine starting wages in apprenticeships, which can be rewarding for those just graduating from high school, as well as the wage scale growth and the benefits that many young people don't immediately appreciate.

We will explore the differences among various programs, from the crafts within construction trades to professions such as technology, health and public safety that are evolving toward apprenticeship models.

I will share stories about the mentors I've met who I still rely on, and who have shaped my thinking and provided guidance that I want to pass on. We will also recognize that there are difficult people and difficult situations that we will always face, and I hope to offer some tips for navigating stuck spaces and avoiding and leveraging risk.

To protect the privacy of certain individuals mentioned in this book, some names and identifying details have been changed. Any alterations have been made with care to preserve the authenticity and integrity of the events described.

I will offer guidance about how to avoid scams in some programs that unfortunately suck time and money from young people but offer little in return.

I will discuss my next steps in entrepreneurship with a developing real estate portfolio, owning over a half dozen properties by the age of twenty-five before graduating from the five-year apprenticeship program.

We will discuss whether we are serious about breaking cycles of poverty and growing financial literacy and creating generational wealth.

While generational wealth can change the trajectory of our neighborhoods, so can public policy. I'll share my priorities as I work as a member of the Maryland General Assembly to improve the lives of young people in communities like those I came from, like Phil.

Actually, his story has a twist.

A few months after starting, he was kicked out of his apprenticeship program after failing too many tests.

If I could do it over, I would have a different conversation with Phil: about the importance of time and not wasting it; about how to overcome the fear of new things and how to embrace the journey. I would have shared that I know we are taught to keep it all within ourselves due to lack of trust or survival mechanisms that the streets of Baltimore instill in us. But those who are successful look for help and seek knowledge from those with learned experiences.

Some of those hypothetical conversations are now written down, in the book you are holding.

Looking back, I had a lot more I could have told him. But maybe I didn't need to.

Phil reapplied, and was accepted, and made it through. His journey took nine years, nearly double the expected time.

But he made it.

I made it.

I know many others can make it too.

CHAPTER 1:

A Hard Introduction to Apprenticeships

I grew up in Baltimore, in a community beaten down by a failing K-12 educational system, a broken juvenile justice system and an adult penal system that is unjust and far from rehabilitative.

The trajectory of my life shifted when I discovered apprenticeship programs, which offer a powerful solution to the historic disinvestment in urban neighborhoods.

While some people learn about these opportunities from a family member or neighbor in the trades, or a high school counselor, I found out about them from my mother, who never gave up on her son.

Renee McCray, affectionately known as Nae-Nae to those close to her, raised me as a single parent with love and determination, spending untold energy to keep me from becoming a statistic in the 1990s and early 2000s.

Nae-Nae was always a fighter, a trait I am proud to inherit. After high school, she took clerical jobs in state government and worked second jobs in the hospitality industry. She attempted to better herself through education—but her journey was cut short by financial hardships. Our home in the Seminole Apartments in Edmondson Village, where I lived until age eleven, was a place of love amid constant struggles.

Sadly, I was a source of many of those struggles.

One week before my eighteenth birthday, I was charged as an adult with possession of multiple firearms and the distribution of narcotics.

I was sent to the Baltimore Central Booking and Intake Center about five miles from my home, a castle-like building that could have been part of a movie set.

As a detainee awaiting trial, I spent twenty-three hours of each day confined in an eight-foot-by-eight-foot concrete jail cell with two beds, a toilet, a sink, and a roommate.

My daily routine: one hundred push-ups, one hundred sit-ups, and one hundred pull-ups. We were allowed one hour outside the cell, for showers, watching television in a 12-foot-by-12-foot recreation room, and family phone calls.

The routine repeated itself the next day and the next. My idle mind was stagnating, its potential unrealized.

Sundays were my favorite. They were visiting day on L-Section, the tier where I was housed.

I remember vividly that Sunday in October 2000, a moment that shifted my life's trajectory from a future fated by a lack of options to a path of fulfillment and financial independence.

I entered the visiting room wearing my green jumpsuit and took one look at my mother, a Black woman in her late thirties with beautiful brown skin, seated in the orange chair at the gray metal table.

Suddenly, I felt a gut punch that hit my core. It felt worse than getting hit in a street brawl. Much worse.

I'd let my mother down. I felt embarrassed to be who I was in front of the woman who cared for me so deeply and spent the last five years hoping and praying I would stay out of trouble.

I faced real jail time for the second time in my life and I was still only a teenager. I was housed with other teens and young adults facing charges of murder, attempted murder or firearm violations, and who were all fifteen or older. We all faced the possibility of not returning home for years or decades.

In the visiting room, I told my mother, "Just let me go."

I thought I was too far gone, and there was no way to change who I was or the world I had entered. I had given up on myself. I truly believed I would be nothing more than a sentence served, or another person shot dead in the streets of Baltimore.

My mother looked me—her firstborn child—straight in the eyes and stated words so deep they still shake me to this day.

"Cory, I am going to keep believing in you until you believe in yourself."

Four Years on the Wrong Track

Shackled, I walked down the long hallway and into my cell, reflecting on the past four years.

My first arrest had come at age thirteen, and I was incarcerated for thirty days on charges of possession of a firearm, a stolen .38 Smith & Wesson revolver that a friend and I had nabbed from inside the home of someone we knew.

I remember the terror as if it were yesterday, being driven away in a blue van in the late evening with other juveniles, my legs and wrists shackled as I was about to spend a month away from my family.

I was truly on my own. I knew I had to give the appearance of being tough, and, during my stay at the Cheltenham Youth Facility in Prince George's County, I learned how to survive away from my family, how to defend myself, and how not to trust anyone.

These are rough lessons for a thirteen-year-old kid.

The same experience took place at fourteen. And at fifteen. And again, at sixteen.

I was arrested again for handgun possession, then for drug charges, then for transporting several guns. I was in and out of juvenile facilities throughout Maryland, from Boys' Village in Prince George's County to Thomas JS Waxter Children's Center in Laurel, the Charles Hickey School in Baltimore County, and the Maryland Youth Residence Center in Baltimore City.

An arrest at age seventeen on gun and drug charges resulted in a ten-month confinement at the Victor Cullen Center juvenile facility in Sabillasville, in Western Maryland.

My mother had come to visit me every weekend, driving up to four hours for a round trip to be with her son.

In those days, I didn't think about the time, gas and money that I took from my family after each incarceration. But I did think about the shame my mother must have felt having to tell her siblings or friends that her son was sent away for crimes.

I did think about the time she brought my grandmother to see me and how it must have hurt her to let her mother know that she had tried her best to raise me right, but was unsuccessful as a mother.

I did think of the times she had to take off work for my court dates and how my decisions could have jeopardized her employment.

She stood by me, year in and year out.

After each arrest and incarceration, I thought I had developed a plan better than the last. But my judgment was cloudy, and the choices awaiting me each time I returned were limited. I still believed that the kingpins who ruled my streets were living happily.

All my life, I had watched my mother struggle, wrestling with a way to remove her family from the perils of inner-city poverty, working twelve to fourteen hours a day. Family members worked multiple jobs just to survive, and then their kids would repeat the cycle.

I knew this wasn't the future I wanted for myself. But as a teen, I was enticed by the lifestyle I saw as I walked home from school, the lifestyle I saw glamorized in rap songs and videos.

But after each arrest, the prospect of longer and longer prison sentences became too real. I was close to giving up on myself.

I turned eighteen on the L-Section in Central Booking, where I had arrived less than a month after my release from Victor Cullen. Now an adult, I was moved to the JI tier among grown men with lived experiences just like mine. But I felt deep down that these men weren't the role models I expected to become.

Then I caught a break in court.

At my next trial date, a prosecutor was offering me and my co-defendant a chance at release because the police had illegally searched my car. My defense attorney, Andy Alperstein, had done his job. Our case was placed on the "stet" docket; we weren't pleading guilty or innocent, but the charges would be on hold for a year in case I was arrested again.

God had already delivered me a second chance, a third chance, and almost ten other chances that I had squandered.

But there would be something different about this one. I was about to take the leap my mother always wanted for me—the one she said in that jailhouse visit that she would wait for.

I was ready to start believing in myself.

Soon after my release, my mother delivered one more gift to me, in the form of a phone call to the Maryland Department of Labor.

Send out, she said, a list of every licensed apprenticeship program in the state of Maryland. She didn't know much about these programs; she just wanted to find something to keep her son out of more trouble.

The list arrived in our mailbox, and she handed it to me.

"Cory, go to each and every one of these locations and fill out applications," she commanded.

How lucky was I that she made that call? Here was a mother under deep duress, grasping at any sort of help for her son.

Already in search of change from within, I was quick to follow her direction and lead.

Meeting the Requirements and Learning Lessons

The parking lot of the Joint Apprenticeship and Training Center was shadowed by a large blue and red building, located off the Patapsco Avenue strip in Southwest Baltimore.

I didn't know what an apprenticeship was supposed to look like, but here I was—willing to knock on the door and figure out the next stage of my life.

Inside, tools and piping filled six or seven classrooms and electrical demonstrations were mounted on the walls.

How was it, I wondered, that such an opportunity was right here in Baltimore, and I had never heard of it?

Baltimore is a city of neighborhoods, and many of us rarely leave the areas we are most familiar with.

At age eighteen, I felt intimidated to walk into this large and unfamiliar building, but I knew I had to do something different if I wanted my life to change.

If you are young, you may need to give yourself a pep talk about stepping into unfamiliar and uncomfortable situations. If you are someone who works with youth, put yourself in their shoes and be sensitive to the discomfort they may feel.

I listened as the instructor took the time to describe for me—someone who just walked in—the benefits of joining the electrical apprenticeship. I looked down at the green sheet of paper that laid out the wage scale. First-year apprentices started off at $12.00 per hour. After completing this program, I'd make $35.00 per hour. And I'd get a raise every year!

Not a single experience during my adolescent years put me on a course where I could envision such a future—double the $35,000 annual wage my mother and aunts made at their government jobs. Was this too good to be true? I had learned in my neighborhood how to spot a hustle, but in this situation, I couldn't understand the angle. The appearance was that I was the big winner, and the organization made all the investment.

At the time, I wasn't even thinking of the substantial benefits beyond wages. I didn't realize the value of employer-paid health care, and the retirement benefits of both a pension and an annuity. I recognize that many young people will feel the same way. But be aware that as you start a family and grow older—as we all do—these benefits will have a direct impact on your lifestyle and financial security.

I looked down the list of program requirements, hoping I would measure up.

First was a high school diploma or GED. Even though I had repeated twelfth grade, I did finish high school at Fairmount Harford Institute in East Baltimore. While this was necessary to be an electrician, some construction trades do not require a diploma or GED. (Chapter 9 contains more about those requirements.)

Second, applicants needed a copy of a high school transcript showing completion of one year of algebra. For electricians and other skilled trades, algebra is important: There's some math behind installing light fixtures and receptacles or conduit bending, for example.

The next day, I went to the Baltimore City Public Schools' headquarters on North Avenue and got a sealed copy of my transcripts. Two boxes checked!

The third requirement was a driver's license, and I had been driving since I was fifteen years and nine months old.

This requirement poses a significant barrier for many young people from disadvantaged neighborhoods who do not generally obtain their driver's licenses while in high school. For anyone considering an apprenticeship in the 11th or 12th grade, it is important to work on this prerequisite.

Why? Some construction sites last for three weeks, some for three months, and some for three years. Employers need assurance that workers can get to jobsites that aren't accessible by public transportation.

While a driver's license is a requirement, owning an operable vehicle is not. Still, during my years advocating for apprenticeships, I have partnered with organizations such as Vehicles for Change, helping to ensure that workers have quality vehicles for a reasonable cost. I have also served on the board of directors for Central Scholarship, an organization that understands the importance of apprenticeships and provides resources to help absorb some of the cost of driver education classes.

Once I knew the requirements and I had met all three, I filled out the application, hoping and dreaming that I would get into this program. At the time, I didn't know this would completely shift my life's trajectory. I just knew that life was about taking risks and trying new things in order to get the full experience.

I feel that's a valuable lesson to pass on. We must encourage young people to take chances, to "fall forward." Any initial rejection should be seen as one more step ahead, rather than a failure. As close friend and supporter Karen Miller often told me, "You miss every shot you don't take, so take the shot."

Preparing for an Interview

After completing the paperwork, I must have called the Joint Apprenticeship and Training Center (JATC) a dozen times to understand my next steps. I wished that, when filling out the application, I had asked for the timeline and steps for the process—but I knew this next step was critical. I would have to sit down for a face-to-face interview to see if I would be accepted.

I was facing a whole series of unknowns, and I was nervous. One thing I knew for certain was that I didn't want to screw things up. But I didn't have a mentor at the time to help me understand the dos and don'ts of interviewing; this was a journey I had to travel on my own. If I could go back, I would have sought mentors who could have identified with this experience—or at least I should have gone to the library and searched for guidance from a book.

After several weeks, I received a call confirming an interview date in February 2003. I don't regret all the calls I made. Persistence is important, and employers respect it, as long as you don't cross over into annoyance.

My mother had taught me several fundamentals that now applied. She always instructed me to dress for the job you want, not the job you have. I picked out a pair of slacks and my best button-down shirt, hoping to stand apart from other applicants. Remember how important first impressions are and that visuals say a lot before you even open your mouth and say a word.

Nae-Nae also taught me to show up on time. For this interview, for a job that could mean earning $12.00 an hour, I wanted to do everything possible. As they say, showing up is half the job. I would learn later in life that showing up on time means showing up fifteen to thirty minutes early for a meeting. If you plan to show up exactly on time, there is a strong possibility you will be late.

I also tried to anticipate and prepare for questions. Unfortunately, with limited experience and a lack of a network, I didn't have much help. In hindsight, I should have consulted a book or two to better anticipate interview questions. For those consulting *this book,* I'm including some of those tips right here!

Here are some standard questions that applicants should be prepared to answer—for an apprenticeship or any other opportunity:

- "What skills and attributes can you contribute to the organization? Give examples of how you have applied those skills and attributes."
- "How do you handle working with difficult individuals? What are some examples?"
- "How familiar are you with the industry? Tell us what you know."

These questions may seem easy for an adult to answer, but they can intimidate someone just out of high school or in their early twenties, especially if they're new to job interviews. Practice, preparation, and role-playing can make a big difference in your delivery or response.

Here are some suggested responses to questions such as those above:

- "You will gain a worker with the ability to follow directions, a strong work ethic, and a passion for learning new things." Most interviewers want to understand how they or the organization will benefit from your work. A positive attitude, willingness to learn, and coming to work on time are strong attributes worth communicating.
- "In life, we interact with a variety of people. I always try to find common goals and look for opportunities to navigate challenges together, while focusing on each person's strengths." It's easy to notice our differences, but seeking to work together creates durable, efficient and effective teams. And teamwork is key in the workplace.

- "While I have never worked in the electrical industry, I am a fast learner and will go the extra mile to be an asset to the organization." No one expects you to know everything, but being teachable is important. The majority of people accepted into apprenticeships have no prior knowledge of the industry, but those who finish have a strong willingness to learn. Of course, you can be a step ahead. Do some internet research and share something of what you learned.

In my own interview on that February day in Baltimore, I was asked why I wanted to join the program, what value I'd bring, my work history, and how I'd heard about the apprenticeship. I breezed through those.

But if I'm being honest, a question about algebra made me stumble.

As an adolescent with some leadership qualities and knowledge from the streets, I learned early how to hustle and respond to authority figures. I was able to answer skill-based questions gracefully. But in the interview, basic algebra tripped me up.

In school, I performed well in math. On this day, I fumbled over a standard question: "If $A = 5$ and $C = 12$, in the equation $A + B = C$, what does B equal?"

I knew B was 7 and answered correctly, but when they asked how I knew, I froze. One of the interviewers asked me to write it on a chalkboard, and even though I'd answered the question right, I realized I was at a breaking point. How was I supposed to write it out? The answer had just popped into my head. This had always been my challenge in school: knowing the answer but not being able to show the work. I fumbled through four long minutes, gave some closing remarks and left.

I walked out feeling less than sure if I would be accepted into the apprenticeship and almost as if I had let myself and my family down. But I also knew I had done everything I could. I still believe if you do your best at that moment, you should always be proud of yourself and your accomplishments!

I kept calling the JATC for several weeks after the interview to find out whether I had been accepted, and the assistant training director, Dave Norfolk, began to expect my weekly calls.

In March or April, I received a call back. I was told that I had done well on the interview, but my application was being waitlisted for the next class, unless someone from this class decided not to accept their position in the April class. I felt defeated, and that I wasn't good enough for the program.

Looking back, I shouldn't have been so hard on myself.

One day, I ran into Dave and his assistant, who were shopping at a Home Depot in the Baltimore suburb of Lansdowne where I was working, not far from the apprenticeship site. I seized the moment. "Do you know by chance if there was someone who didn't accept their position in the April class?" I asked Dave. He told me that he would check.

At 4:00 p.m. on the day of the orientation, I received a call on my cellphone saying, "If you can get here by 5:00 p.m. today, you can join the April class."

Driving to the parking lot and walking into my classroom for orientation that April day gave me one of the best feelings. No one else knew that I was accepted an hour before the orientation.

Each training course had up to 100 students, based on the anticipated needs of the industry. It didn't matter whether I was number one or number one hundred. I was now at the same starting line as everyone else in the April class, and ready to give it my all to get to the finish line.

Life Lessons Through Apprenticeship

Engage, Educate, Execute

In each chapter you will find this Life Lessons section, which serves as a summary, checklist, and tips to develop and implement your plan for success.

- **Have you mapped all apprenticeship programs located in your city, county, or state?**
    » Find the organization that tracks and distributes information on apprenticeships. For the state of Maryland, this information was housed with the Maryland Department of Labor.
    » Note the apprenticeship programs that spark your interest and the proximity of programs to your home.
    » Identify the wages, benefits, and requirements to be accepted into each apprenticeship program you are interested in.

- **How well are you prepared for your apprenticeship interview process?**
    » Identify the expectations to be placed on the apprentice while matriculating through the apprenticeship. (Basic math, algebra, etc.)
    » Consider what to wear on interview day.
    » If possible, identify people within your network familiar with the program and ask them about their experience.
    » Practice answering the questions provided earlier on paper and out loud.

- **How will you follow up after the interview process?**

- **Remember, persistence is key, and follow-up is important.**
    » Following up two weeks after the interview is respectful.

> If you don't receive an answer during the first follow-up, ask during the call or visit when it is appropriate to follow up again.

My goal for Chapter 1 is to share the lowest point in my life and show how my trajectory shifted from a life of incarceration to one of fulfillment and financial freedom. If you are questioning if the apprenticeship path is right for you, I hope this chapter provides a blueprint to understand, identify, apply, and gain acceptance into an apprenticeship of your choice.

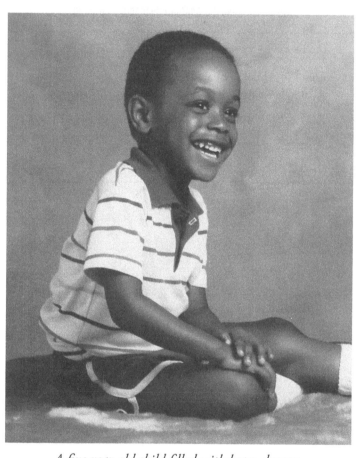

*A five-year-old child filled with hope, dreams,
and an unfiltered view of the world.*

CHAPTER 2:

Earn While You Learn

Throughout my teenage years, I hustled.

I made a little bit of cash to satisfy the moment, but held total disregard for my future. Like many others in my situation, I just couldn't imagine it.

Yearning to make money, I spent a lot of time during twelfth grade on the corners of Pennsylvania Avenue and Laurens Street, one of the busiest drug markets in West Baltimore during the late nineties.

I was out before 9:00 a.m., peddling marijuana and then straight cocaine to those addicted to drugs who were heading to work. The same rush took place in the afternoon when the same customers, chasing their next high, clocked out at 5:00 p.m.

You could say the IBEW wasn't my first apprenticeship. I already had a notion of what it meant to "earn while you learn."

On the streets of Baltimore, I was earning about a thousand bucks a day selling cocaine, thinking it might add up to an escape from poverty. I was learning about the teamwork needed to set up efficient structures and avoid arrest. I was gaining an understanding of the skepticism I needed to avoid falling victim to the sob stories of addicts. I also learned that no one was irreplaceable.

But I knew it wasn't a way forward. And in an instant, a much better way to earn and learn appeared.

Starting in the construction trades through an apprenticeship provided a solid wage immediately, with a clear path for growth over the ensuing five years.

It also met a goal of improving my education, although there would be lots of testing ahead with little room for error.

Still, I had some initial apprehension.

I believe we all wrestle with two voices: doubt and risk.

My "doubt" voice was telling me that this was a hustle and that I needed to find out the gimmick before they got the angle over me. Like on the streets.

The reality is that there was no hustle. Employers throughout Baltimore, I came to realize, valued a trained workforce that can contribute to their bottom line. Apprenticeship-trained workers were in demand.

As for the "risk" voice, that one was easy. It asked me what I had to lose by going down this path. The answer? Nothing.

In April 2003, the day I was accepted into the apprenticeship, my starting wage was $12.00 per hour. If I stayed with the program without incident, the wage scale would rise more than three dollars an hour each year, until I would earn $25.63 an hour as a fifth-year apprentice, and then $32.93 hourly the next year as a journeyman. [Today's rates are much higher, with journeymen earning $47 an hour.]

I couldn't believe it; the certainty of money like this seemed too good to be true.

By the time I turned twenty-five, I would be making almost $30 an hour. I would be not only the highest-earning person in my family, but the highest paid in my immediate network—apart from the more accomplished crooks in my neighborhood. The wage formula gave me a clear goal and a clear path to get there.

An additional $3.89 an hour went toward health care and wasn't coming out of my direct wages. This benefit may not be important to most young people walking around healthy and feeling invincible. But soon enough, I had my first child, Kennedy—and the importance of quality health care hit home. Kennedy would be covered by my policy as long as I worked 350 hours over a three-month period.

Health care was just one of the benefits I could now receive. Union negotiators had the foresight to envision that one day we would need to retire from the profession. An additional $3.65 per hour was contributed toward a pension. At the time I had never heard of pensions – a guaranteed income stream when I reached a certain age. It was a huge plus.

Those same leaders knew that a pension and Social Security might still leave a gap in retirement needs, so they added an annuity—where an additional $2.65 per hour was contributed and invested toward retirement, with more guaranteed income.

Altogether, if a worker contributes thirty to forty years of their life to a trade, they can retire with dignity. The average electrician can work steadily during their career and retire as a millionaire!

So while most twenty-year-olds would look at the earnings of a second-year apprentice and see $15.36 an hour, I quickly realized that the total value of the package was 60 percent higher—or more than $24 an hour. What a game-changer for those of us who grew up in neighborhoods where many had no retirement plan!

At the start, I didn't need to know anything about electrical work. A good attitude and an appetite to learn were the two things I needed to bring to the table.

The apprenticeship office gave me a tool list and recommended a good pair of steel-toed boots for the jobsite. The night before I started work, my mother took me shopping for tools, but we didn't shop for footwear. I showed up the next day in Timberland boots—the fashion norm for my generation. I also favored oversized jeans and shirts two to three sizes too big.

But soon enough, I traded fashion for safety. Those steel-toed boots offered way more protection, and my loose clothes posed a danger around equipment that could snag or grab them.

With one call to the apprenticeship program letting them know I wanted work, they facilitated the process with a pool of electrical contractors that had an agreement with the school.

The first contractor I worked for was Gill-Simpson Inc., the electrical company helping construct a parking garage at 210 St. Paul Place in Downtown Baltimore.

The job began with one foreman, a journeyman, a second-year apprentice, and me. I was lucky enough to work on this job from start to finish, for about seven months.

On the jobsite, I learned how to heat and bend PVC piping, a fundamental of electrical wiring, and how to install lighting fixtures and receptacles. I also pushed the broom and learned how to get breakfast or lunch orders for my colleagues working on the job. While these may seem like trivial tasks, I learned that everyone has a role in getting the job done.

I also got to know people in other crafts (carpenters, plumbers, elevator constructors, and more) and observed their work.

We were paid every week, and I was ecstatic to receive my first check as an electrical apprentice: more than $300.

I would also soon learn that not only did I have the ability to work Monday through Friday from 7:00 a.m. to 3:30 p.m., but in our craft we have the opportunity to work overtime when necessary.

I picked up every Saturday possible, with pay for those hours at one-and-a-half times my normal wage. In addition, any hour after eight hours per day was paid at one-and-a-half times our hourly wage.

I was also able to work two Sundays a month on this jobsite, which paid double time. As that garage rose, some weeks I worked fifty to sixty hours. I couldn't believe it; in my first year, some of my paychecks were $400 to $500 and more. They called me an "overtime hound." I wasn't sure in the beginning how long this experience would last; I thought it was too good to be true.

I continued with Gill-Simpson Inc. throughout the first year of my electrical career. Other projects included the Sparrows Point Wastewater Treatment Plant, the Baltimore Sun's Sun Park printing press, and the CSX Curtis Bay coal piers.

We took jobs at the National Aquarium and inside Baltimore public schools. We even constructed intercom systems for McDonald's drive-throughs across the city. I gained so much knowledge during my first year, and I still take pride when I drive past that garage and the other jobsites I worked on. Waking up every weekday morning, arriving on the jobsites early, placing my green hard hat on my head and tool pouch on my waist—I can truly say that these small actions helped to make me the person I am today.

On Learning

Let's turn to the learning side of the "Earn While You Learn" apprenticeship equation.

For the first three years of my five-year program, I attended one day of classroom instruction every two weeks—known as Day School. Every other Wednesday, I sat at a desk and learned about required basics like Ohm's law, parallel and series circuits, and more. The last two years consisted of electives such as security systems, fire alarm installation and cable splicing.

In Day School, we received a stipend to cover pay lost while not being on a jobsite. During the first year the stipend was $50 per day; it rose by $10 in each of the next two years.

In public school, the idea was almost forced upon us that college was a necessity, and that my family needed to pay for it – perhaps going deeply into debt. I never thought I would be in a situation where an organization paid me to go to school.

This opportunity exists because there are employers who value a trained workforce. Monthly student loan debt for those who have sought a four-year degree is about $300, while under the apprenticeship system, you can graduate debt-free—and, in the case of many such as myself, accumulate savings and investments as well.

My class was made up of twenty-five students, who happened to be all men. Over five years of taking classes together and sometimes working on the same jobsites, I would forge lifelong relationships with these "brothers."

Our first-year instructor was a Black man named Horace Ellis whom I held in the highest regard.

He was one of the first men I knew who wore a suit every day to teach—in front of a class of mostly White men. Usually, when I saw men in my community wearing suits, it was because they were going to a religious gathering.

Standing about 5'10" tall and solidly built, Horace was a strong leader who cared deeply about his students. He taught us not only to take pride in ourselves, but also to appreciate the history of the industry we were training for and the value of the organization.

I was one of only five Black men in my class, and it helped me to see people who looked like me in leadership positions. Seeing Horace command a room gave me the confidence to know that one day I could do it too.

As a first-year apprentice, the on-the-job training was easy, but I must be honest: The classroom instruction was not my strong suit. I had not applied myself to learning strong study habits as I stumbled through high school. I was also a couple of years removed from school. By the time I started my apprenticeship, much of the information I had learned in middle and high school had been lost.

While the schooling was free, we had to pay for our books. However, if we received a 93 percent average during the year, that expense was reimbursed. It took a couple of years for me to reach that goal. In the first year, I found myself struggling with the same discipline challenges as in high school, trying to figure out a way to get by.

An intense sense of pressure was built in. In each of our class days, we were tested on the topics we had covered during the previous class period, two weeks earlier. If we failed three tests we were out of the program. No debates. No do-overs.

I passed the first test, but by the time we got to the eighth one, I had already failed two. I had no more margin of error.

Recognizing what was at risk, I confided in Horace that I couldn't fail out of this program; my family was counting on me to find direction, fulfill my potential and launch a successful career.

He informed me that he had been conducting free coaching classes on his own time for students who needed it.

Why, I asked myself, had I not been taking advantage of this all along? With all that was at stake, and the specter of failing one more test and flunking out of the program, I did what I had to do and found myself with several other students in coach class.

I quickly realized that my testing struggles weren't due to a lack of intelligence, but were the result of not using information and skills taught during my public education years. Coach class quickly changed the course of my schooling, and it also strengthened my relationship with Horace. I think he respected me more because he saw how hard I worked to stay in the program.

Within the first few weeks of coaching, I watched several colleagues fail out. One by one, Horace called them into the hallway outside the classroom to inform them that they had failed a test. On the third test failure, they gathered their things and headed down to the main office, not to be seen again.

I was determined to escape that fate.

In class, we learned things such as Ohm's law, formulas and how to read the electrical code book. We practiced hands-on applications such as pipe bending, wiring, and motor controls—skills we might not be exposed to on a jobsite. Nonetheless, you are expected to know how to apply them as a journeyman.

The school was in a state-of-the-art building that enhanced our knowledge about the electrical industry and its future. There were nearly a dozen rooms, each with unique features. We had a classroom specifically for learning about how to wire fire alarm systems, and another dedicated to motor controls for industrial areas. In the security classroom, we learned about window and door contacts and security cameras.

I did not fail another test in year one.

In my second year of schooling, my instructor was Neil Wilford, a serious, almost wonkish instructor committed to his craft. I had built solid study habits, had received my raise and knew what was at stake. An even stronger sense of solidarity among classmates was growing, and instead of coaching class, several of us formed study groups to ensure no one was left behind. This was a year when none of us failed out of the class. I passed every test.

In my third year, led by Larry Ryan, a retired, no-nonsense instructor, I challenged myself even further, and reached the 93 percent average need to receive the book reimbursement. I remember as the last test approached, I was tempted to give in and let things slide. But I buckled down, determined not to let all the previous hard work go to waste. We were also conditioned to know what to expect. The school had two years' worth of financial investment poured into us, and they wanted to see us succeed.

My fourth and fifth years, in which I attended night school, were a little different. Instead of attending school one day every two weeks during the day, we took our electives twice a week at night, from 5:00 p.m. to 9:00 p.m. We engaged with many more of the other apprentices during night school because the building was fully used.

Looking back, the "Earn While You Learn" model was perfect for me. It gave me the ability to address my immediate need for income, while also obtaining an education. While I was initially under the impression this was a hustle, I soon learned that this legit opportunity exists for all trades, no matter whether you wish to become a carpenter, plumber, operating engineer, steamfitter, laborer, painter, ironworker, roofer, boilermaker, etc. All provide opportunities where wages meet instruction, while developing an engaged and trained workforce.

I walked away from the five-year apprenticeship with an education in the electrical industry and wasn't saddled with college debt when I obtained my journeyman license with the IBEW. It can take decades to pay off college debt, depending on the loan amounts, but I left the apprenticeship with multiple vehicles that were paid for, homeownership, and multiple investment properties obtained during the five-year schooling period. The IBEW apprenticeship is a blueprint and model for how to build generational wealth.

If there comes a time when I am no longer participating in the electrical industry, my understanding and knowledge of the trade will always remain. The skills will always be valuable, either to earn a wage or even fix up a home.

Grasping the "Earn While You Learn" model was a pivot point that helped with my decision-making. It filled my immediate needs and set the stage for a successful and secure future. This has truly been a journey, but more importantly, a gift.

Life Lessons Through Apprenticeship

Engage, Educate, Execute

- **Explore the differences in wage scales between the various crafts:**
  - » Always consider the starting wage of the crafts you have chosen, and the incremental increases offered during your apprenticeship tenure.
  - » While health care isn't always on the minds of young, healthy people entering the apprenticeship, as you grow your family, having the best insurance, especially when you don't have to pay for it, will be a welcome asset toward happiness and wealth building.
  - » Consider whether the apprenticeship offers a pension, annuity, or 401(k). These investment perks will increase in importance and value as you move through your career.

- **Schooling is the second half of apprenticeship; consider the tools to be prepared:**
  - » Evaluate whether the apprenticeship program you are considering is a three-, four-, or five-year program. On average, most apprenticeships are four-year programs. A shorter apprenticeship may put you in the workforce faster, but a longer one may provide even more skills and expertise.
  - » Don't be afraid to seek help from instructors or classmates during your apprenticeship tenure. The strong bonds established can help you throughout your career. Never forget that your network is your net worth.
  - » Always put forth a strong effort; instructors pay attention, and this goes a long way when you face a crunch and are in need of grace.

- **Preparing for your first day on the job:**
  - » I highly recommend having a good pair of steel-toed boots. Construction sites can be dangerous, and it is always best to be well prepared.
  - » Regarding your tool list, my approach was to purchase the most important tools necessary to do the job up front, then invest in one additional tool a week. Tools are expensive and should be considered an investment. The tools you need will depend on the craft you choose. I would be remiss if I didn't mention to invest in quality tools whenever possible to ensure longevity and durability.

> My goal with Chapter 2 is to highlight both on-the-job training and schooling. The first day on the job comes with a level of anxiety and nervousness, but in the end, I walked toward the opportunity and was able to make a good wage and prepare myself for a new skill set, all while building lifelong relationships. The next chapter will explore what you can do in high school to prepare for the apprenticeship experience.

Cory V. McCray, far right, at age eighteen, with siblings and other family (L to R: nephew Chris; sister Charmaine; sister Danielle; niece Charlese; brother Bernie).

CHAPTER 3:

Preparing for Apprenticeships While in High School

Most kids in Baltimore and across the country attend just three schools while growing up—elementary, middle and high school. They benefit from the stability that comes with familiar classmates, teachers and surroundings.

Not me. I had the unfortunate experience of attending seven different public schools before the eleventh grade, and I was removed from five of them for behavioral challenges.

My schooling started on a positive note, at an elementary school that provided experiences I will always treasure. My mother had not enrolled me in kindergarten due to work obligations and a lack of child care options as a single mother.

I began first grade at Rognel Heights Elementary in a special education class so I could catch up. A caring teacher, Ms. Lyde, helped me surpass my academic goals. The principal, Sarah Horsey, created a nurturing learning environment that allowed students to thrive. I made the honor roll and excelled year after year, with phenomenal teachers such as Ms. Solomon, Ms. McCoy, Ms. Allen, and Ms. Linear.

Things changed in middle school. I was removed from West Baltimore Middle School near the end of sixth grade, and from Chinquapin Middle School in the middle of seventh grade. I enrolled next in Winston Middle School near my grandmother's home, where I stayed through the eighth grade. My repeated expulsions were not for academic reasons, but mainly for behavioral issues and my inability to develop in overcrowded learning spaces that lacked rigorous curricula and standards to hold my attention.

I am pretty sure I have always had a wandering mind that was never challenged enough, and my entrepreneurial spirit and constant yearning and questioning "why" went unnourished. I knew that my mother couldn't afford for me to go to one of Maryland's fine four-year colleges—or even a community college. Neither of my parents had a college degree. So I never formalized the idea of higher education or thought that it was possible or realistic.

I had little exposure to job occupations and couldn't think of a career beyond those imagined by many Black boys—sports and hip-hop. I was good at neither.

While I didn't know anyone who worked with their hands, I did walk past the auto mechanic shop in Edmondson Village every day while heading to sixth grade and occasionally said hello to the mechanics who fixed my mother's car. Deep down, I identified with them, and could envision myself in that occupation.

Three Baltimore high schools prepared students for trades: Mergenthaler Vocational-Technical, Carver Vocational-Technical and Edmondson-Westside. I chose Edmondson-Westside, because it was close to my mother's home on Edgewood Street, and I had a cousin who went there who could help me adjust. I signed up for the automotive class, but was removed after four months for fighting and cutting class.

By that point, I was staying out all night, running away from home, drinking liquor and more, and my mother understandably grew fed up. So I went to live with my grandmother—my father's mother—on the east side of Baltimore and enrolled in Northern High School.

Moving between homes with my mother in West Baltimore and my grandmother in East Baltimore would be a pattern in my life during my teenage years. I lasted one year at Northern High School. I began selling drugs and only went to school to have fun, hang out with friends, and sell marijuana to classmates.

After my removal from Northern, I was sixteen and on my last stop at the alternative school called Fairmount Harford Institute, nicknamed "The Tute."

During my entire public-school journey, I only failed one year, which was the twelfth grade. But I took night and weekend classes, and received my high school diploma without any sense of next steps.

I still don't know how or why I graduated when most of my friends that I was hanging out with at the time were dropping out in the tenth or eleventh grade. There was just something about knowing that I was capable, and it was pretty easy to get it out of the way.

Luckily, I had a mother who never gave up on her son and steered me toward the course of exploring the apprenticeship route after high school.

As I have looked back on my K-12 public education and then my completion of a five-year apprenticeship, I often think about the information and resources that could have helped young people like me—those for whom college might not be the best or most practical choice, and those who want challenging and fulfilling careers.

As an adult who has become a public servant focused on improving lives in Baltimore, I have conceived and implemented several initiatives that have made the pathway from school to apprenticeship more achievable.

In each case, I've enlisted partners and used experiences from my own background to increase knowledge of exposure to trade-focused training programs, and to make them more accessible for kids coming from the same neighborhoods that I grew up in.

Here are four of them:

Hands-On Weekend Classes for High School Students in Partnership with Apprenticeship Programs

Knowing the value of apprenticeships and my limited knowledge of them while growing up, I asked myself what I would have liked to have known as a high schooler. I figured I could complain about the local school system needing to fill these gaps, or I could do something about it myself.

I chose the latter.

In 2019, I reached out to the principals at Carver and Mergenthaler, and asked them if they would be willing to participate in a weekend program that would expose their students to apprenticeships. Carver's Shionta Somerville and Craig Rivers at Mergenthaler were immediately interested in the concept.

I then enlisted Neil Wilford, training director at the Joint Apprenticeship and Training Center (JATC) Local 24 and the second-year instructor at my electrical apprenticeship program. He helped configure a workable idea using resources available at the center.

We established a program that would run for four Saturdays, for six hours each session.

The classes would be hands-on: Students would bend conduit, learn about the different gauges of electrical wires, and get training in how to wire light switches, receptacles, and lighting fixtures.

The training center would donate construction material, and the instructors would volunteer their time.

The participating high schools provided transportation for the students who needed it each weekend to ensure they arrived on time and had a safe passage back home. Up to 20 juniors and seniors from each school who were seeking more information about the electrical profession were chosen.

We also walked the students through the apprenticeship application process, and familiarized them with the instructors and staff.

On the last weekend, we welcomed and encouraged parents to attend to ensure that they, too, understood the application process and the requirements for employment.

The entire experience put smiles on many faces—from students and parents to apprentices and instructors.

After the first few sessions, you could see the nervousness and reluctance ease as the students grew excited about learning a new skill.

We provided lunch, and saw that sharing a meal broke down more barriers. Students were able to have conversations with adults about future plans and the possibility of joining the profession. It was gratifying to watch that exposure and engagement build comfort and confidence.

I remembered how intimidating it was to walk into the training center and request an application for an industry that I didn't know much about. That barrier was now removed for these students, who built relationships with the training director and other instructors.

Seeing and interacting with apprentices who are close in age and possibly grew up in the same neighborhoods as our participants gave them tangible evidence that their goals were within reach.

Apprenticeship Tours for High School Students

After creating the weekend program, I wanted to do more. I asked myself why high schools conduct college tours in the fall, but not apprenticeship tours. That's a gap I thought I could help fill.

I brought the concept to my local school district, and when they failed to move on the idea, I reached out to friends Cassie Motz, executive director of CollegeBound Foundation, Jimmy Tadlock and Melissa Hypolite, who thought that it was a great idea. They agreed to cover the transportation costs if we could make it happen.

CollegeBound Foundation is an organization that helps Baltimore students achieve their higher educational goals. Cassie has helped the organization become more active in assisting students seeking alternative pathways such as apprenticeships.

I then contacted training directors in the region to see if they would like to participate. All were welcoming. We were able to partner with electricians, carpenters, plumbers, steamfitters and operating engineers to create a one-day tour of multiple apprenticeship programs in 2019.

After that, I got in touch with all of the high schools within the footprint of my legislative district—Reach Partnership, City Neighbors High School, Dunbar High School, and the National Academy Foundation (NAF). All of the principals were excited and receptive.

From those four schools, the initiative has since expanded to seven schools—some outside of my legislative district—and is now held twice a year.

I am proud and grateful that the CollegeBound Foundation has taken the lead, arranging scheduling, permission slips and transportation. The Baltimore-D.C. Metro Building Trades pays for lunches, ensuring that access to food isn't a distraction to learning.

The visits include activities such as virtual welding and simulations for heavy equipment operations. Students have been exposed to how to frame partition walls and install drywall, while developing relationships with training directors.

While many juniors and seniors on these trips may not join the building trades, it is valuable for them to explore all opportunities and make the most informed life choices, and I know that these initiatives contribute to those decision-making moments.

Each year, more school guidance counselors have attended, looking to understand better what the building trades can offer their students. And while the majority of students have been male, a growing number of females have been participating—a welcome development.

Hands-On Skills Competition for High School Students Interested in Apprenticeship Programs

In Maryland, jurisdictions with trade schools organize skills competitions for high school juniors and seniors to show off what they have learned during their coursework.

Students compete in everything from cosmetology to mechanics, building trades, culinary arts and more. For several years, I have been a Maryland judge for SkillsUSA, giving me a unique opportunity to spot local Baltimore talent and help steer the future of these promising young people.

It quickly became clear to me that many trade schools outside Baltimore had more resources, and their students won their respective competitions more often. These competitions were important for giving participants a spotlight and a leg up as they moved through their training and into careers. Many of the sponsors were companies that might be looking for future talent.

After I saw the advantages of well-resourced schools, I could better advocate for the programs and resources for Baltimore City Schools.

All in all, I believe these competitions provide great opportunity to build character, persistence, team building, and exposure to expectations of future employers.

Expansion of Legislative Scholarships to Be Inclusive of Career and Technical Education (CTE)

Every year in the Maryland legislature, the members of the Maryland State Senate and House of Delegates can appropriate scholarship funds to their constituents seeking higher educational opportunities. When I first joined the legislature in 2015, this was only offered for enrollment in community colleges or universities in Maryland, and never to registered certificate programs with the Maryland Department of Labor.

Apprenticeships have never been a partisan issue; it is an area where Democrats and Republicans agree that expanded opportunities will help restore the middle class. Still, most legislators have no direct experience in blue-collar occupations or in how apprenticeships work. In fact, I believe I am the only person in the 188-member General Assembly who graduated from a registered apprenticeship in Maryland. And

I am possibly the first person to be elected who completed a registered apprenticeship program!

After I joined the legislature, I sought to expand the use of legislative scholarships to cover apprenticeships.

In 2018, my friend Kevin Hornberger, a Republican delegate from Cecil County, helped spearhead this idea into law with bipartisan support. Now, apprentices can apply to their delegate or senator for a scholarship to help cover course costs, fees, and room and board. The resulting conversations over this initiative have helped move apprenticeship programs into more equitable footing with our two- and four-year institutions of higher learning.

I have also taken these conversations into the private sector through my volunteer leadership activities.

Staying Up to Date on Apprenticeships

There is a quote that I constantly remind myself of: "You don't know what you don't know."

If I were reliving my high school years, I would map out all of the apprenticeship programs near me and familiarize myself with the locations of these respective crafts. I would seek insight from guidance counselors, looking for tours of these facilities—or asking them to read this chapter and help set them up. Every city or county has local building trades and a training facility.

Each trade will have different application processes, graduation requirements, math requirements, or driver's license requirements. You want to be as prepared as possible, so understanding the requirements will be vital for your success.

For example, if your state has time limits on when those with a learner's permit can drive, this would be a perfect thing to know before filling out the application. If your school does incorporate apprenticeship tours for high school students, make it a point to seek out and introduce yourself to training directors or instructors who can help you. Let them know your interest and how you are preparing to enroll in their training program after graduating from high school.

Apprenticeship programs are evolving in order to better bring in a new generation, so inquire whether they have initiatives engaging high school students or if they provide opportunities to advance one year ahead in the apprenticeship program.

My apprenticeship (IBEW Local 24) started an initiative just two years ago that gives future apprentices in their junior and senior year the opportunity to take online courses, which gives them a head start in classroom training. Upon completion, they start off as second-year apprentices.

This initiative saves time, and puts more money in students' pockets through the higher wage scale. Most apprenticeships belong to national umbrella organizations that share best practices and curricula, so there is a strong possibility that if one state is doing something, others will soon follow.

If you are attending an apprenticeship with any costs like tuition, mandatory fees, or books, seek out scholarship information to see if there is available funding. If you are lost on where to look for apprenticeship funding, check with programs that are offering funding for community colleges and higher educational institutions. There is a growing realization that students who are pursuing alternative career paths need assistance in finding and accessing funding.

Lastly, if there are weekend or summer opportunities to become a helper within the craft that you are interested in, seek them out. These positions have historically been offered to those with family members, friends or neighbors within the craft, but now that you know about these opportunities, you can reach out yourself.

These are just some of the resources I wish that I had known while in high school, which would have better prepared me for my apprenticeship journey.

I want you to know what I didn't know. And I hope you use this information.

Life Lessons Through Apprenticeship

Engage, Educate, Execute

- Make a plan to research all the apprenticeship programs in your jurisdiction:
  - » Contact your local Department of Labor to request a list of registered apprenticeship programs in your jurisdiction.
  - » Upon receiving the list, draft your own list of the career paths that you are interested in, and mark their physical location and contact info.
  - » Research the website for their training centers and check to see what those requirements are.

- Consult with your guidance counselor or career pathway counselor:
  - » Reach out to guidance counselors at your school to see if there are any apprenticeship tours in your junior and senior years.
  - » After researching the enrollment requirements, start working toward making a checklist to see what you need to accomplish.
  - » Check to see if the apprenticeship program of interest has initiatives set up for those in high school to accelerate their apprenticeship experience.

- Research scholarship opportunities:
  - » Some apprenticeship programs have costs associated with them. Some programs that offer higher education scholarships are moving in the direction of helping with these costs.
  - » Contact your local elected officials to see if they have funding to assist with apprenticeship career pathways.

> My goal with Chapter 3 is to highlight the preparation that can take place during the latter years of high school. This includes all the information I wish I had known before embarking on the apprenticeship journey. The next chapter will explore the costs associated with various apprenticeship programs and how to find programs free of charge.

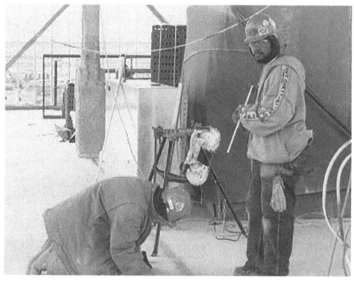

As a fifth-year apprentice, installing four-inch conduits on the roof of the National Institutes of Health building with my journeyman, Chris Gray.

CHAPTER 4:

How Can an Apprenticeship Be Free?

I learned early in life to be skeptical of things that seem free. I thought that any person appearing to be your friend may prove to be, as the saying goes, a wolf in sheep's clothing.

The streets of Baltimore teach you to be on the watch for wolves, and they also instill those wolf-like traits in many of us.

At age eleven, I moved from Edmondson Village to my grandmother's home in Northeast Baltimore. It was a less restrictive environment. But the wolves were still there.

At my grandmother's, I spent most of my time hanging outside, playing pickup basketball and football, wrestling with friends, chasing girls, and getting into small-time mischief.

But on one hot summer morning about two years into my stay, my neighborhood friend Trevor knocked on my grandmother's door, asking if I could come outside and hang out.

In those days, I would often leave the house before noon, jump on my bike and hang outside until 10:00 p.m. or later.

My grandmother or older sister (who was living with us) knew the dozen or so neighborhood boys I was hanging out with, or perhaps their older siblings.

That day, as we were walking around the neighborhood, Trevor uttered a sentence that disrupted our routine and would change everything.

"I know," he told me, "how to get a gun."

Never once did I ever think about owning or needing a gun. At that time, it wasn't the life I was living, and I was just trying to have fun as a kid. We had never gotten into this level of trouble before.

My gut reaction was hesitancy, but I admit I was not much of a leader at the time. I went with the flow and followed his lead.

We walked to Trevor's friend's house to steal his dad's gun, which Trevor had scoped out the day before.

I had never met the boy or seen him around the neighborhood, so I wasn't sure how Trevor knew him. Trevor pretended to use the bathroom while I stayed in the living room, talking with the friend as if everything were normal.

When Trevor came back down the stairs, he gave a head nod—a signal that he had nabbed the weapon from a bedroom and was ready to leave.

We headed toward a vacant house with trees in the yard about five minutes away, a hangout spot we called the "hole."

Trevor pulled out the silver .38 revolver, and I was astounded. I had never been that close to a gun and didn't know what to expect. We played with it for a while, trying to figure out how to load the bullets. Then we pulled the trigger, sending three shots each into the air, running away in case someone called the police.

Over the next few days, we convinced one of our older friends to purchase bullets from the local gun store. We ran around recklessly for the next week, shooting into the air and trying to look cool in front of our friends, showing the gun to anyone we could.

After about two weeks of incredibly irresponsible behavior, the police knocked on my grandmother's door one evening at about 9:30 p.m. They wanted to question me about a stolen gun.

I had learned from the streets to keep my mouth shut so I acted as if I didn't know what they were talking about. They mentioned Trevor's name and details about what had happened. I wondered how they had all this information, but still didn't say anything. Even if I had wanted to give them the gun, it was at Trevor's house.

So that night, I went off in handcuffs, not fully clear about what would come next because I had never been arrested or placed in a police car.

I spent the night on a metal bench inside a beige jail cell at the Northeastern District of the Baltimore Police Department, listening to conversations between officers. I waited for my grandmother or mother to come and get me. But they never did.

I learned a few weeks later that the boy's father realized his firearm had been stolen. He reported it to the police with a suspect in mind: Trevor. But my friend told police that I was involved in the theft and I had the gun.

While Trevor was charged and released to his mother in less than eight hours, I was sitting in a jail cell by myself, with no one picking me up.

My mother and grandmother were frustrated with the trouble I had been getting into around the neighborhood, and with my removal from several middle schools.

This incident, they say, was an escalation to a problem that they couldn't control. They thought I should learn a lesson, which would come from being locked up in the juvenile system with other troubled youths. And they believed Trevor's story—that I had the gun.

That was a hard reality to face and it cut me to my core. I was in the worst trouble I had ever been in, and it seemed to me as if my family didn't care about me anymore.

The next morning, I was loaded into the back of a police wagon on my way to the Mitchell Courthouse in downtown Baltimore, where I would see a magistrate handling juvenile cases.

The whole process was scary and new, but something I would become familiar with over years in and out of the juvenile justice system.

I sat in a large courthouse holding cell with multiple juveniles ages eleven to seventeen, chained at the wrist with shackles on my ankles. I was terrified, and I wondered why my mother didn't come to my rescue on the worst day of my short life.

Juveniles flowed in and out of the holding cell, taking their turns in front of the magistrate, learning if they were to be released or detained. When it was my turn, it was clear there was no parent or guardian coming to get me. The magistrate ruled that I would be detained until my next scheduled hearing, in thirty days.

That evening, all the juveniles who were still in the cell—including me—were loaded on a blue bus and driven for an hour to the place where I would spend portions of my teenage years: Cheltenham Youth Facility, also known as Boys' Village, in Prince George's County, Maryland.

Over the next month, I figured out how to survive on my own, incarcerated for the first time at the age of thirteen.

At Cheltenham, I learned to protect and defend myself if I needed to. I witnessed, for the first time, boys and girls who had it far worse than me. For some, the safest space was inside a juvenile facility.

After two weeks, my mother visited me during Sunday visitation hours, restoring my hope that someone back home loved me.

Trevor ended up telling the truth—that he had the firearm. He turned it over to the police, and it was eventually returned to its original owner.

I was released at my next hearing, which my mother and other family members attended. I reestablished my relationship with my mother and grandmother after they both learned that I wasn't lying and didn't have the firearm.

That experience, like many others growing up in an urban jurisdiction, made it clear that even people you consider friends don't have your best interests at heart. Some would see you incarcerated to save themselves.

I came to learn that nothing was free in life. I learned to be suspicious of those looking to give you something because, more than likely, they were trying to take something off your plate. The wolves were hungry. This was still my attitude when I approached my apprenticeship.

Money for Real

As I sat in the training center filling out an application for an electrical apprenticeship, I read the green card handed out with the form, outlining the wages for those accepted into the program. It read:

- $12 / 1st-year apprentice
- $15.18 / 2nd-year apprentice
- $18.27 / 3rd-year apprentice
- $21.42 / 4th-year apprentice
- $25.77 / 5th-year apprentice
- $32.86 / Journeyman Wireman

Working forty hours a week, a journeyman would make more than $68,000 a year. It was 2003, and I didn't know anyone in my family or neighborhood who made that amount. I thought about all the things I could do with those earnings. Heck, even if they stopped my pay at $20 an hour, I would have been happy!

There was other information about health care, and pension and annuity benefits—but I didn't know much about that or how it would impact me in the future, so I ignored that information. [As we discussed in Chapter 2, that's a mistake. All young people should recognize the value of these benefits.]

They also talked about schooling, which initially didn't interest me but was necessary to get to that prize: the $32 hourly wage. For the first three years, I would be paid a stipend to attend one day of classroom learning every two weeks.

But I kept asking myself how much this training would cost me. They kept saying that it was free and that they would be paying me to work on the job to receive training and attend school for class instruction.

For two years, I waited for the "gotcha" moment because this wasn't my reality or the reality of anyone from my neighborhood. I pored over every document I needed to sign, looking for the gimmick. I talked to others in the program looking for the hustle. But I found nothing.

I came to realize that when businesses invest in a well-trained workforce, their companies grow more profitable and competitive on large commercial and industrial jobs. This was how employers were able to pay attractive wages, and the Joint Apprenticeship and Training Center was able to pay stipends.

Over time, I learned that I had joined an apprenticeship of an electrical labor union, and I began to understand how labor unions had been established. This was not discussed much in the schools I attended.

I learned that the wages, health and retirement benefits, and working conditions I enjoyed were collectively bargained between the labor union and the signatory electrical contractors. This allowed those contractors to deploy the best-trained workforces, with limited turnover and fixed labor expenses.

The International Brotherhood of Electrical Workers (IBEW) is not the only craft that doesn't charge a fee to participate in the apprenticeship. Free union apprenticeship programs raise the bar and compel nonunion programs to apply the same approach to attract and retain the best talent.

Other Models

While the apprenticeship program I joined had no tuition cost (but still required me to pay for expenses like books and clothing), there are other models and examples to be aware of. These include split costs; costs paid by the apprentice; and on-the-job training programs.

Let's review.

Split-cost model: The split-cost model is most common to nonunion apprenticeship programs. Employers come together to implement their own training program and curriculum or partner with a community college or other institution. The employer recognizes the value in training the workforce but believes the apprentice has some responsibility to finance the experience. Typically, employers pay between 60 and 80 percent of costs, and the programs run three to four years.

Full-cost model: The full-cost model normally only includes smaller employers that don't have the capacity to subsidize schooling. The employer may also partner with a community college or apprenticeship program. This model isn't always sustainable because once the apprentice attends school, they learn of peers participating in no-cost or split-cost programs, and may seek to switch.

When working with a nonunion employer in the split-cost and full-cost apprenticeship programs, the contractual obligation is only met when you're working. If, for some reason, the apprentice is laid off due to economic downturns, health concerns, or downsizing, that contractual obligation is normally void. Young employees could work to find a new employer and renegotiate the terms of payment for apprenticeship program costs, or could seek work with other craft contractors, but they may not have a relationship or contract with the original apprenticeship training program. This should be taken into consideration when evaluating apprenticeship programs.

<u>On-the-job training</u>: While these programs may sound attractive, there is a major risk that the apprentice could be taken advantage of. In my situation, I was guaranteed a wage increase if I advanced each year, completing education and passing tests. But with on-the-job training, employers may know that if the apprentice does not complete schooling, rules of a contractual obligation don't apply, and the wages may not rise. Aspiring workers may be stuck at a lower wage for years.

In many states, training programs must register with the respective labor department and receive accreditation. The state agency ensures completion of training hours and classroom instruction before awarding an apprenticeship certificate or craft licensure.

In on-the-job training programs, young workers may not enjoy the full benefits of a contractual obligation overseen by the state. I have always been leery of the types of employers that only participate in on-the-job training, because the people that they prey on tend to be low-income, within the reentry community, or unaware of the standards in place.

While I enjoyed the benefit of a no-cost apprenticeship program and consider it the gold standard, the other options can be practical in nonunion settings.

Please note that the costs I refer to are specifically for tuition. For most, if not all, apprenticeship programs, workbooks are needed for education requirements. For me, the expense was up to $400 a year, which could burden a first-year apprentice.

I give the reader the same guidance my mom gave to me: Find all the apprenticeship programs in your area registered with your local Department of Labor. Narrow your list to the crafts that interest you. Review the top three programs in those crafts and evaluate the cost models. Early research can save time and money, and help you figure out which program is best for you.

The skepticism and apprehension that I had before entering the apprenticeship program came from my lived experiences, but I soon learned there was no hustle.

Instead, there was a mutually beneficial relationship. I and other apprentices needed to pass tests and stay committed. And by the time we reached our third year, it was rare for someone to be removed. Both the apprentice and the program were vested in mutual success.

Life Lessons Through Apprenticeship

Engage, Educate, Execute

- Narrow your list of apprenticeship program choices to three crafts:
  - Research the websites for different cost models and structures.
  - Is the class instruction held at night or during the day?
  - Does this program pay stipends for class instruction?
  - How many days during the week will classroom instruction be held?

- Apprenticeship referral versus employer solicitation:
  - How does the employer referral system or process work?
  - Review the contractual obligation with the apprenticeship training program or employer.
  - Is the apprenticeship program of choice a credentialed registered apprenticeship with your respective Department of Labor?

- Walking toward your blessings:
  - Some things are going to be scams. Research the opportunities to converse with people who participated in the program to see if it fits you.
  - If you do meet a blessing, be sure to inform others of the opportunity because "you don't know what you don't know."

My goal with Chapter 4 is to ensure you are well-versed in the different cost models and structures of various apprenticeship training programs. The next chapter will dive deep into my weaknesses and successes in building study habits to complete the apprenticeship journey, along with the lessons I wish I had known along the way.

*Speaking to students about different functions of electrical work, including cable splicing.
(Credit: Kiwauna "Kiki" Seldon)*

CHAPTER 5:

Building Better Study Habits and Surviving the Apprenticeship

At age sixteen, I received a ten-month sentence inside Maryland's notoriously troubled juvenile justice system. A judge consolidated several drug charges I had racked up over several months—possession with intent to distribute— and we settled on a plea agreement that resulted in the most serious punishment I had received in my young life.

The judge and my caseworker weighed sending me to an out-of-state facility, but my mother advocated for a stay within Maryland to lessen the burden of long-distance travel for visitation.

Her position prevailed. But my family and I knew that I was going to be gone for a while this time.

My first stop was the Cheltenham Youth Facility in Prince George's County, also known as Boys' Village. I had been there before for shorter stays, but this time was different. After an hour-long drive from the Mitchell Courthouse in Baltimore, I arrived at the juvenile facility in the evening and was placed in cottage number six, home to the oldest and hardest juveniles on the campus.

Burgundy was the color of our uniforms in cottage six. We needed an identifier so staff could easily spot us in case we tried to escape or were in areas where we didn't belong.

All across the facility, I saw kids I knew from East and West Baltimore and others that I had met during past incarcerations. Some were friends, and others were foes. There were hundreds of juveniles at Cheltenham, and most came from the two majority-Black jurisdictions in Maryland: Baltimore City and Prince George's County. I had never spent much time outside of Baltimore City before. It was surprising to see and hear the differences in speech, clothing and musical taste of people who lived just thirty miles or so apart.

On the first night and during many nights after, I replayed in my head advice that a childhood friend, nicknamed Dime, had given me years before after an earlier arrest: "Don't let none of those boys play with you."

When incarcerated, there's always someone who will try you, test you—to see if they can dominate you.

And that happened during my first week at Boys' Village.

Carr was a teenager who had been arrested for carjacking. He was around my age, and a little bigger than me. And he was running his mouth about me for no reason.

One afternoon early in my stay, Carr and I were together with dozens of other kids in a large holding room with no staff.

I had had enough of his lip. I did as I was taught: survive. I punched him square in the mouth so everyone in the day room could see not to play with me. We grappled for about five minutes until staff rushed in and pulled us apart. As punishment, we were each locked down in cells for 72 hours.

While being locked down, you got your breakfast, lunch, and dinner meals served in the cell and ate them by yourself. They let you come out for showers separately when everyone else was done for the evening. All I could do was exercise and wrestle with thoughts about how I got myself a ten-month sentence that was just starting, not knowing how the rest would turn out. I was frustrated by the mistakes I had made. I was missing my family and wondering what was happening back home.

I was also thinking about the advice from Dime, and was fixated on what I was going to do to Carr once we were let out.

After three days, we were both released from lockdown and found ourselves in the same bathroom that morning, cleaning up. Carr was brushing his teeth, and at that moment, both of our instincts told us we were supposed to fight again.

So we did. And we both got another 72-hour lockdown. Then it happened a third time.

Our total confinement reached nine long days. That was enough. We reached an unspoken agreement that we respected each other enough to let it go, appreciating the human interaction we got outside of the staff that served meals and monitored our showers during confinement.

I would participate in a couple more of these skirmishes before the planned transfer to my next placement at the Victor Cullen Center, about 70 miles outside Baltimore in Sabillasville, Maryland.

I arrived there more hardened and less tolerant of even the smallest sign of disrespect. Within two weeks, I got into an altercation with Foye, a younger teenager from West Baltimore, trying to earn his stripes with members of a gang that I was beefing with.

The fight was so violent that when they started a new experiment to gather all the worst troublemakers in one cottage to effectively fight among themselves for survival, I was chosen as a prime candidate. By isolating the worst offenders, staff could attempt to rehabilitate others who seemed more committed to improvement. For three weeks, I was housed with the roughest juveniles, kids who may not have had family or any incentive to make it back home.

Then I caught up with one of my friends, Hike. He reminded me that I had a strong network of family and friends back home. Why was I getting into fights with people who had little reason to leave, for whom this facility was probably the best thing they had? Hike was telling the truth.

I had too much to return home to, and I was wasting my energies with young people I would have ignored in Baltimore. Improbably, Hike helped me identify a problem and work toward a solution. I decided my goal would be to get back to a supportive family and decent life.

With fresh focus, my behavior improved, and two weeks were shaved from my six-month placement. I appreciated the perspective and guidance shared by a friend. I returned home earlier than planned.

Solving Problems

Some of the same principles that helped me build discipline and gain focus during incarceration would help me during my apprenticeship.

Sadly, my Baltimore City Public School experience put me at a major disadvantage. I never exerted much effort in school but moved from grade to grade and received a diploma by clearing a low minimum standard. I was surrounded by other teens who lacked motivation or ambition to find alternatives to escape our social situation.

That school system was sending hundreds of graduates yearly into the workforce without the skills needed for success, or basic resources like financial literacy and mentorship.

There were different types of students in my apprenticeship class. Some had a family member in the IBEW and knew what to expect. Some came from school systems outside Baltimore, where they may have had more educational success. And then there were those like me without the skills they needed for success.

In my class, twenty-seven apprentices were accepted, and five of us were Black. About five apprentices dropped off in the first six months due to test failures, attendance problems, or lack of interest in the career path. The rest, including four of my Black colleagues, would hang on for the entire five-year program.

Despite the success I was experiencing in on-the-job training with my electrical employer, Gill-Simpson, class instruction during my first year was rough.

Almost immediately, I struggled with basic algebra and electrical concepts. I failed two of the first seven tests. I knew that I needed a quick change to survive, because failing a third test would mean my ejection. I needed to figure out how to pass five consecutive exams to stay on my trajectory and avoid letting my family down again.

That year, I was blessed to have an instructor named Horace Ellis, as we reviewed in Chapter 2. As a young Black male growing up in an urban jurisdiction, entering a space dominated by older White males, Horace provided an example of what could be possible if I completed this program. Horace wore a suit every day to work, reminding us to dress for the roles we want.

Horace held everyone to the highest standards and didn't cut any slack, regardless of race, age or gender. In Baltimore City Public Schools, it always seemed as if they were lowering the standards instead of expecting us to meet our full potential. But Horace would accept nothing less than excellence, and I started to feel as though I could meet his expectations.

Horace pulled me aside after my two test failures and let me know that he didn't believe I was reaching my maximum potential. He asked me why, if I was having issues with the curriculum, he had never seen me in his coaching class. The truth was, I never saw myself as someone who needed coaching or extra help, and was never exposed to it in high school. Having nothing to lose and everything to gain, I took Horace up on his offer.

Twice a week, I would drive my tan 1987 Chrysler New Yorker to the training center after getting off my jobsite.

At the first class, I saw I wasn't alone; there were a number of first-year apprentices more than likely in the same situation as me. I would stay for an hour or two until I was able to understand the objectives for that class. Sure enough, I passed my next test. And the next one and the next. I was focused and benefiting from coaching class.

Later on, I grew comfortable enough to form study groups with fellow students, ensuring that we understood the concepts, passed the tests, and, perhaps most importantly, left no one behind. I must admit that while growing up on the streets of Baltimore, I only looked out for myself and my team. The apprenticeship was teaching me that there was enough opportunity to go around. Sticking together would help us all win. Structures like coaching class and study groups were instilling skills and changing my perspective in ways that would guide my life from then on.

With my newly learned study habits, I saw a 20 percent improvement in my test performance in the second year. Soon, another goal was in sight: If students got a 93 average on the dozen or so tests each year, book money—one of our only out-of-pocket expenses—was reimbursed. During my third year, I tried to reach this incentive. It was trying, exhausting, and frustrating, but I got there and earned my book money. In fact, I was only one of three apprentices to hit that mark during our entire five years!

Here are some of the lessons I learned during my apprenticeship:

- The first rule to resolving any issue is recognizing the problem.

- Solving problems comes from exploring options and even writing down possible solutions.
- Once you identify the issue and explore possible solutions, think about how to create a habit and commit.

Recognizing the Problem

It's tempting to blame others for our challenges instead of evaluating the situation and looking at what we could be doing better. As a first-year apprentice, I knew that I wasn't equipping myself to succeed in weekly tests that would get me across the finish line. I didn't have a basic understanding of needed math concepts, but I was trying to mask the holes in my knowledge by not asking questions.

It wasn't until Horace, my instructor, told me that I was in danger of failing out of the electrical apprenticeship that I realized I needed help and a plan. Don't let things get this far; take the first step in recognizing the problem.

Options on Paper

When we recognize a problem, a window opens, and it becomes incumbent upon us to take action. An easy way to take a small step forward is to write down possible options or solutions. You are now making physical and mental moves—sending a thought wave to lock in and focus on these possible solutions.

You can use your written options as an accountability tool to help you reflect on and meet your goals. You can post the paper somewhere and use it as a reminder of what needs to be accomplished. One of my greatest secrets about putting things in writing is that once you accomplish each goal on that paper, you can reflect on your successes and turn small wins into big victories. All wins are contagious and breed momentum. If you are successful, you are creating good mental vibes and raising the chances of meeting future goals.

Habit and Commitment

After acknowledging problems and writing them down, the real work begins with implementation. Many people have great ideas, but the ones who are successful implement their plans.

Building the courage to attend coaching class was one step, but it was the second day and the third day that were even more important, because I was building a habit. Once you build a habit, you start to question why you would not be doing what you know you are supposed to do.

With time, we can all create new habits, build disciplines and create a sustainable framework for meeting success. I went from coaching class to creating study groups and engaging with my peers—taking my new habits to the next level. When you change your behavior and mindset, you can see the board more clearly and identify other opportunities.

Life Lessons Through Apprenticeship

Engage, Educate, Execute

- **Recognize the Problem:**
  - » The first step to solving any issue is acknowledging that it exists. Reflect on your challenges and identify the areas where you need improvement.
  - » Be honest with yourself about your struggles and limitations. This self-awareness is crucial for growth and progress. No matter where you start, you have the power to change your trajectory.

- **Explore Your Options:**
  - » Write down possible solutions to your problems. Use this as a tool to focus your mind and visualize your path forward. Consult with mentors, instructors, or peers who can offer guidance and support. Leverage their knowledge and experience to find the best course of action.
  - » Don't be afraid to ask for help. Surrounding yourself with supportive individuals can make a huge difference. Embrace the journey and view every challenge as an opportunity to learn and grow.

- **Build Habits and Commit:**
  - » Understand that change requires consistent effort. Start by taking small, manageable steps toward your goal. Develop a routine that includes regular study sessions, attending extra help classes, and forming study groups. These habits will build a strong foundation for your success.

> Strive for excellence in everything you do. Set high standards for yourself and work diligently to meet them. Remember, the key to success is perseverance. Commit to your goals and stay dedicated, even when the journey gets tough.

By following these principles, young adults can navigate their apprenticeship journey with confidence and determination. The support of mentors, instructors, and a dedicated routine can help overcome challenges and build a successful future.

Recognize your potential, seek out support, embrace the journey, and commit to excellence to thrive and reach your full potential.

The goal of Chapter 5 is to help young adults recognize and address the challenges they face during their apprenticeship journey by building self-awareness, exploring viable solutions, and developing consistent, effective habits. By understanding and implementing these strategies, they can overcome obstacles, leverage support systems, and commit to a path of excellence, ultimately achieving success and personal growth in their chosen field.

Speaking to students at the Joint Apprenticeship and Training Center about my journey into the apprenticeship program. (Credit: Kiwauna "Kiki" Seldon)

CHAPTER 6:

Gaining Mentorship Through Apprenticeships

As I grew up, my big brother and uncles served as mentors who showed me the ways of the streets. With their guidance, I learned how to survive and hustle. They weren't knowingly steering me down a wrong path; they were teaching me as best they knew.

I particularly looked up to my older brother Bernie, and always tried to emulate him. Everybody in our neighborhood knew Bernie; he was loved and respected in the streets. Bernie taught me valuable lessons: Never let anyone take anything from you without a fight, and don't turn your back on family. He would come to my rescue or sacrifice his safety to protect mine time after time.

When I was eleven, I moved in with my grandmother in Northeast Baltimore after getting into small-time trouble at my mother's home in Edmondson Village. Before then, I had been sheltered from the outside world by my mother's protection, so when I gained the freedom to wander outside and explore the neighborhood, I took full advantage.

During the summer of 1993, I rode my new green and black mountain bike—a prized possession—all over our neighborhood and adjacent blocks, hanging out with friends my age who also benefited from caring parents and didn't get into much trouble.

A local shopping center contained a Giant supermarket, a liquor store, convenience stores with arcade machines, and a local pizza shop called Marino's that was a prime gathering spot. I was familiar with everyone, whether they were my age or teens like my brother and sister.

Even the older folks and store owners knew me because my grandmother frequented the stores for food and lottery tickets. At that point, I hadn't gotten into any real trouble, just small-time mischief. I was just out having fun. I would quickly learn that what I defined as fun was different for others, especially those who had grown up harder than I did.

One summer morning around 11:00 a.m., I rode my bike to the shopping center and ran into Eric and his friend Marco. I knew Eric from the Northwood Elementary School basketball court, but didn't know Marco. Both were in eighth grade, one or two years ahead of me. Marco asked to check out the new bike, which my grandmother had bought for me just a few weeks earlier. I was alone, waiting for friends to come outside to hang out as always.

Eric seemed to know what was going to happen. But I didn't see it coming. With my bike in his hands, Marco laughed and told me I wasn't getting it back.

I had no idea how to respond to such a brazen act.

Growing up with mostly women and no real male figures in my life to teach me how to box or wrestle, I was ill-equipped for a confrontation. All I could do was walk away with tears rolling down my cheeks, not knowing what I was going to tell my grandmother and imagining how my summer would be ruined by the loss of the coolest toy I ever owned.

I headed for my big brother's house on Woodbourne Avenue, and told Bernie what had happened. My brother kept a .38 revolver handgun on his nightstand, and I suggested we use it to get my bike back. He taught me an important lesson: It's best to know how to use your hands and defend yourself.

We walked back down Hillen Road toward the shopping center, and Marco and Eric were still there. Bernie was seventeen and much bigger, and Marco and Eric were terrified as I pointed them out; they dropped the bike and started running.

Bernie caught them, and I was expecting to see my big brother deliver a pounding, or at least start a two-on-two battle that our side would win with ease.

But that's not what happened.

Bernie pulled Marco aside, and made him fight me right there. Marco was scared, but Bernie assured him it would be a fair fight.

I, too, was frightened. How could my brother, whom I had enlisted to protect me, make me brawl with someone who we both could see was bigger and older than me?

It didn't take long for the skirmish to go as I predicted. I was slammed around the first time, lying on the ground and ready to quit. But Bernie made me go back a second time, and then a third. After the fourth time, Bernie said "enough" and Marco and I shook hands.

I was destroyed and embarrassed, with mud on my clothes from repeated body slams and tackles, but Bernie had let everyone know not to mess with his little brother.

In tears, I walked with my bike to my grandmother's house, upset and confused about why I had to fight someone I knew I couldn't beat. But Bernie talked to me all the way home. He told me never to let anyone take something from me without a fight. He didn't care if they were older or bigger. The point was to not be scared to fight and throw a punch. If others know that one person can take something from you, it is only a matter of time before everyone would come.

This was the type of the hard lesson that shaped me in Baltimore, teaching me perseverance and to face my fears. I never saw Marco again after that day, but I knew how to handle him or someone like him in a similar situation.

A New Group of Mentors

I entered my apprenticeship armed with lessons learned from mentors on the streets. I would soon gain a new set of life skills from a new set of guides.

From day one on my first jobsite, I was assigned to work with a journeyman wireman. Each apprentice works with at least one journeyman and sometimes two or three, depending on the job. This is done primarily for safety, with the ratio of apprentices to journeymen dictated by state regulations.

These journeymen taught me not only about the electrical craft, but also about the fundamentals of the workforce.

I learned about the importance of showing up on time—which really means arriving ten to fifteen minutes early. One journeyman, Henry Jefferson, liked to show up forty-five minutes early so he could read the newspaper before the start of the workday. I sometimes carpooled with Henry and jokingly asked if we could get there thirty minutes early instead of forty-five. He resisted.

These journeymen would become key figures in my life as I earned while I learned. From them, I gained insights into everything from grooming and good work habits to how to save and invest.

Let me introduce you to three key mentors: Ed Sheck, a journeyman electrician with my first electrical employer; Mike Rolley, whom I met through my second employer; and Frank Voso, with whom I worked at IBEW Local 24.

Ed Sheck

For my first two years, as discussed previously, I worked for Gill-Simpson Inc., a contractor for industrial and commercial projects throughout the Baltimore region. I met Ed Sheck during my third project. He was the foreman while I worked at the CSX coal piers off Keith Avenue. Our crews were small, between four and ten people, and I was the only apprentice on the project for about seven months.

It was an outside job, starting at 7:00 a.m., But Ed always arrived by 6:30 to make sure everything was in place for our team to operate efficiently. He didn't talk about it, but he didn't have to; I learned from his actions.

Ed showed me that a real leader gets in the trenches with his team. I had seen this on the streets, but it was different at a worksite. When we were installing light poles and lighting fixtures, Ed showed me how to run a piece of equipment called a Ditch Witch to dig trenches, and how to use a truck and booms to install the large poles.

If someone didn't show up for work one day, Ed immediately stepped in to do the task. Seeing that type of leadership helped me take on larger roles than most first-year apprentices, accelerating my growth.

On that job, I kept myself guarded and didn't joke around much. But we would learn more about each other on future projects. When we installed intercom systems for several McDonald's restaurants, I worked harder than I ever had in my life. The profit margin was so low that every minute mattered. I saw how much energy Ed was putting in, and I tried to match it. I applied what I like to call my "chess strategy," thinking three or four moves ahead of the journeymen, anticipating what tools and materials they needed next, and how to make their jobs easier.

Ed knew how much I liked to make money, and scoped out overtime opportunities for me. We would put in eight hours on our job, and then head to another job that was behind schedule and put in another eight hours there. He drove the company truck to the second job, letting me rest. With this extra work, weekly checks reached up to $900—compared with the regular $300 or $400 for a first-year apprentice in 2003—fat with time and a half or double time as I gained more real-world experience.

To be sure, I would run into some not-so-great journeymen throughout my career, but I was always prepared for the next job because of Ed's lessons.

Mike Rolley

My journey took an exciting turn when I met Mike Rolley while working for my second employer, Brown & Heim Inc., a contractor doing work for Northrop Grumman at multiple facilities. We spent most of our time at the site closest to Baltimore/Washington International Thurgood Marshall Airport. One of Mike's areas of expertise was real estate, and I learned much from him on that topic.

I didn't talk much about my life outside the job, detracting attention from my co-workers. That was a lesson learned from the streets: Keep your mouth closed, move in silence, and survive.

But after a few months of listening to Mike talk about rental property that he owned, I decided that this was something I needed to learn. I had already purchased my first home on Woodlea Avenue, and figured to buy a rental property from the money that I saved up as a second-year apprentice.

Mike taught me about different types of loans and purchasing strategies, and I also began reading about real estate to learn the industry.

Mike gave me one priceless nugget of knowledge that I remember to this day. He asked me if I had a line of credit, and I didn't know what that was. He explained the concept of a home equity line of credit, or HELOC. I picked up more books and then went out and applied for credit lines on all three of the homes I owned at the time. This system gave me the opportunity to purchase all of my future homes with cash and pay the bank back after acquiring a mortgage.

Mike gave me the ability to take the first step and the courage to see my future. Because of Mike's mentorship, I would own more than a half-dozen homes at age twenty-five. I'll be exploring more of my experience as an entrepreneur in Chapter 10.

Frank Voso

A new chapter of my life began when I met Frank Voso at IBEW Local 24. Frank was a second-generation member of the union, with several family members who also belonged. Frank showed me the value of strong family connections. I had grown up with brothers and sisters, a mother, grandmothers, aunts, and uncles who loved me. From Frank, I learned how to raise a family and how to be engaged as a male figure.

I watched as Frank paid for all of his children to attend private school, something unfamiliar to me. Frank valued education and was willing to work hard to provide what he thought was best for his children's success.

I also learned from Frank about the value of exposing your children to different experiences—particularly through vacations. He would plan those vacations with direct and extended family members months in advance.

I had never been on a plane before age twenty-five and did not leave the country before I was thirty-five. Learning from Frank's experience, I would make sure that my children would have a different blueprint than what I had been given.

Two of Frank's nephews joined the local union immediately after high school graduation, sure about their career paths. Frank consistently guided and encouraged them, and made sure they had a network of friends and mentors to navigate the industry. Part of the reason I am writing this book is to make sure that young people growing up in circumstances similar to mine can see a path forward and can plan accordingly.

Frank always talked about his father and other ancestors, appreciating how much they contributed to the growth of the local union. I didn't grow up with this level of connection to my forebears, but I was listening and learning moves I could make when I had children. Through Frank, I would gain better understanding of my own lineage.

While I didn't imitate Frank entirely, I embraced the values that were important to him: education, exposure, experience, and keeping the stories of the past alive for future generations.

I believe the story of my childhood shows that anyone can overcome their circumstances. The adults and family members around you today are most likely teaching you important lessons, in the best way they know how.

I appreciate my mentors—both on the streets and on jobsites—who taught me so much about work ethic, financial management, leadership, and family values.

As you reflect on your own mentors, remember that it's okay to seek guidance from different people for different aspects of your life. Engaging with mentors can help you avoid mistakes and benefit from their experiences.

Life Lessons Through Apprenticeship

Engage, Educate, Execute

- **Identify and Engage with Potential Mentors:**
  - Reflect on individuals in your life who have provided valuable guidance.
  - Consider mentors from various backgrounds—both personal and professional.
  - Reach out to potential mentors and express your desire to learn from their experiences.

- **Understanding the Role of Mentorship:**
  - Recognize that mentors can teach you more than just technical skills; they offer life lessons.
  - Value the diverse perspectives and experiences mentors bring to your journey.
  - Be open to learning lessons in work ethic, financial management, leadership, and personal development.

- **Maximizing the Mentorship Experience:**
  - Actively seek feedback and apply the lessons learned in real-world situations.
  - Emulate positive behaviors and practices demonstrated by your mentors.
  - Share your growth and progress with your mentors, showing them the impact of their guidance.

> My goal with Chapter 6 is to highlight the invaluable role of mentorship in shaping one's personal and professional journey. By sharing my experiences and the lessons learned from my mentors, I aim to inspire you to seek out and engage with mentors who can provide guidance and support. This chapter underscores the importance of learning from others to navigate challenges, build resilience, and achieve success. In the next chapter, we will explore working with difficult people, navigating challenging situations, and building discipline through reflection and better decision-making.

Explaining devices and wiring for homes to Baltimore City students in 2024 at the Joint Apprenticeship and Training Center. (Credit: Kiwauna "Kiki" Seldon)

CHAPTER 7:

Working with Difficult People and Navigating Difficult Situations in an Apprenticeship

There are moments in life when your past catches up with you. But as you're navigating the storms that come from a reckoning with the consequences of actions, know that winter doesn't last forever.

At age eighteen, I was facing my second adult charge as a juvenile, when I had been home for nearly a year and was trying to turn my life around.

I was back with my mother on Edgewood Street in Edmondson Village, working multiple jobs and maintaining a steady relationship with my then-girlfriend, now wife, Demetria. I was determined to change my path. But I had been in the drug game for five years and was well-known in my neighborhood and others. It was hard for people to believe that I was genuinely walking the straight and narrow and giving up the game.

One night, after getting home from work and spending an hour with Demetria in East Baltimore, I drove my tan 1987 Chrysler New Yorker home, turned off the radio, and walked toward my house.

Suddenly, a masked gunman jumped out of the bushes two houses away from where I lived. I heard the chilling words, "You know what time it is," a common phrase on the streets during my time, and a prelude to a robbery. I had stopped carrying illegal handguns while home on bail, and now here I was with a weapon in my face and no way for me to respond.

My street instincts kicked in. I realized I had a couple of steps on him, and if I could take off, my chances of staying alive would increase. I did some quick mental calculations as if I were solving a math problem: Are they kidnappers? Are they stickup boys?

I ran as fast as I could down the steep slope of a hill, weaving in and out of cars, hoping to avoid the bullets I expected to follow. Halfway down the block, I let go of the heavy black Army fatigue coat that was slowing me down. At that point, I was surprised I hadn't been shot or heard any gunshots. I stopped running, realizing there was only one attacker behind me.

Summoning my courage, I turned back and wrestled with him, managing to get the gun out of his hand.

It was a revolver. I pointed it at his chest and pulled the trigger. Click. Click. Click. The gun was empty. No bullets.

As we struggled, another man appeared. He knocked me to the ground, and together, they fled into the night. Exhausted and in disbelief, I made my way back home, trying to wrap my head around how close I had come to being killed, or how I might have killed my attacker if the gun had been loaded.

I desperately rang the bell, and my mother opened the door to find me lying on the porch. She pulled me into the living room as my chest heaved, pleading to know what trouble I had gotten myself into this time. In shock, I couldn't respond.

Moments later, the doorbell rang again, and the police were standing there, holding the coat I had dropped during my escape. As they asked me questions, they accused me of being the robber, based on information in the jacket that had led them to my home.

I eventually convinced the police that I was a victim and not a perpetrator, and they left. But my mother was in doubt. Given my past, she found it hard to believe I wasn't involved in something shady, especially considering how quickly police arrived with their accusations.

This attack was karma. I thought about all the times I had robbed others for a gold chain, jacket or shoes. The attacker could have been anyone from my past who thought I was still involved in illegal activities.

This was a crossroads moment. I could hunt down the robbers and exact revenge, letting the incident derail the changes I was trying to make in my life. Or I could continue on the path I had recently turned to, figuring out how to shift my life in the right direction.

I was angry. Angry with the police and my mother who were accusing me, and angrier with the robbers who had confronted me. But ultimately, I realized I could only be upset with myself. I was the one who made these past choices. If I hadn't sold drugs in the past, no one would have been waiting outside my home in the middle of the night.

I also thought about how blessed I was not to have had a firearm that night. Would anyone have believed it was self-defense from an eighteen-year-old currently on bail for handgun and drug charges awaiting trial?

I was just beginning to realize that life was precious, and that I had value. I would not seek retribution. I would not revert to old habits.

To this day, I'm not sure how I survived that night or why I made the choices I made in those moments. But I walked away a better person, putting distance between myself and the karma of the streets. I weathered the storm.

Integrity and Professionalism

Embarking on careers, particularly in the construction industry, young workers will inevitably encounter difficult people and challenging situations. These tough experiences are crucial learning opportunities that shape professional and personal growth.

I will share three pivotal stories that illustrate the challenges I faced during my apprenticeship and the skills I developed from them.

I believe there is an eighty-twenty rule in life: 80 percent of the people you encounter are striving for excellence, but the remaining 20 percent are trying to bring the rest down.

As a fifth-year apprentice, I was working for a contractor by the name of Enterprise Electric on one of the largest jobs of my career. The project at the National Institutes of Health Bayview Campus was one of the most significant construction jobsites in the Baltimore region at the time.

There were more than 300 electricians working on three different shifts, starting at 7:00 a.m., 3:00 p.m. and 11:00 p.m. I worked the morning shift with the majority of the electricians.

After the first week, I realized the journeyman electrician that I was teamed with wasn't there to teach or to work. He was in the 20 percent, and absolutely was not delivering eight hours a day of work. He left early for lunch and returned late, and was sometimes nowhere to be found.

With four years of on-the-job experience under my belt, I could read blueprints, bend pipe, pull wires, and complete other foundational practices. I had learned well from good craftsmen, like my mentor Ed Sheck.

I plowed ahead on the necessary tasks without the assistance of the assigned journeyman, building a reputation as an apprentice with a strong work ethic and solid know-how.

What I didn't realize was that the senior leadership of the company was watching and respected my ambition. They trusted me with projects that strengthened my skills.

It would have been easy to slack off and take advantage of the employer. The journeyman certainly opened the door for it. But I was committed to the profession, and knew the right thing to do. I had already learned the critical thinking skills to navigate a situation like this, while maintaining my integrity.

Resilience in the Face of Adversity

During my second year in the apprenticeship, I encountered a difficult situation where I did fall short.

I was working with a Gill-Simpson journeyman, Kris, who wasn't keen on the work habits that I had been taught by Ed and others. He wanted me to slow down and stop making him look bad.

This direction didn't make sense, so I ignored it. It went against everything that I was learning, and it put me in danger of being reprimanded.

So Kris decided to haze me. On the CSX coal pier jobsite, we used a company truck to move around the campus. At the end of the day, we would drive to a common wash area to remove the black soot before getting into our personal vehicles. One day, Kris decided to leave me at the washroom. He jumped in the truck and returned to the work trailer where we started and ended the day, forcing me to walk a half mile, fuming.

When I got to the trailer, it was locked up and all of my co-workers were gone for the day.

A colleague twice my age, who was supposed to be leading by example and contributing to my career development, had disrespected me by deserting me on the jobsite.

My street instincts kicked in, and I spent the entire night planning retribution. I chose not to inform the foreman (my mentor Ed Sheck). I was festering and convinced myself that

I only had one choice: I was disrespected, and I had to turn it up a notch—the behavior I used to practice on the street.

That next morning, we both entered the work trailer before 7:00 a.m., along with another journeyman, Leroy. I played it cool, giving no sign that anything had happened the previous day. As the clock struck at the top of the hour, Kris headed to our work truck, a white Ford F-150.

I had not said a word. I just got into the passenger seat, closed the door, and immediately put my hands around Kris's throat.

He screamed for help, and Leroy ran to assist. Leroy split us up and asked what had happened. I explained that Kris had left me at the washroom the previous day. He made the excuse that he thought I was at the work trailer, even though my car was still in the employee parking lot.

Leroy informed Ed, the foreman, about what had taken place that morning and things were very tense as we went back to work.

I later learned that management knew Kris had a habit of being a jerk, and found the encounter more comical than serious.

I was pulled into the office by training director Dave Norfolk. I acknowledged that I wished I had made different choices and had possessed the strength to walk away.

Dave reminded me of the first day that we had met in that Home Depot, and the urgency I had showed to be part of the apprentice program. I needed to put that same type of energy into my decision-making, he told me, warning that things could go in the wrong direction if someone filed a complaint or tried to elevate the situation.

Dave was guiding me, not threatening me, making it clear that as an apprentice I had a lot at stake. I may not have triggered the incident, but I escalated it and faced the harshest repercussions. He reminded me that I had more to lose than the journeyman.

I walked away knowing that there were people in my corner attempting to guide me, while also learning that I bore responsibility for my actions. I needed to learn not to make such mistakes again.

Dave would leave me with words that are still meaningful to me today: "A smart man learns from his own mistakes; a wise man learns from others."

I think of this saying in all of my interactions, and I encourage others to do the same.

Facing New Challenges with Courage

Sometimes a new opportunity becomes a challenging situation.

After completing my first five years as an apprentice, I was ready to transition to the role of journeyman wireman. I had done exceptionally well with all three of my employers, working multiple jobs, collecting overtime, and building a sizable nest egg in savings and investments.

Still, I had doubts. I continued to ask myself if I had the skills and drive needed to be successful in this craft, even as the opportunities multiplied. I had been invited even before graduation to join the staff of the Joint Apprenticeship and Training Center as a part-time instructor teaching elective courses at night to fourth- and fifth-year apprentices. I was also invited to become a business agent for my local union, making me just the second African American on a staff dominated by White males over the age of fifty.

These new responsibilities were a bit daunting, but I had learned not to let fear take control of my mind. I was now walking toward the things that I had been afraid of, letting go of the stress of things not in my control. This philosophy has made life easier, and new opportunities have continued to arise. Situations that create fear, I have learned, also carry the most purpose and thoughtful living.

Lessons Learned from Adversity

Each story above illustrates a facet of dealing with adversity, and can be distilled into these key lessons:

- Integrity and professionalism: Upholding your values and maintaining a strong work ethic, even when others around you do not, can set you apart and earn the respect of those who matter.
- Resilience in the face of adversity: Overcoming difficult situations requires mental strength and a commitment to goals, even when the path is unclear and obstacles seem insurmountable.
- Facing new challenges with courage: Embracing new and daunting situations can lead to significant growth and unexpected opportunities.

Through a variety of experiences, I've learned that the key to overcoming difficulties lies in our ability to stay true to our values, persist through tough times, and embrace opportunities for growth. By maintaining a strong work ethic and a commitment to personal development, we can turn obstacles into stepping stones and setbacks into comebacks.

Life Lessons Through Apprenticeships

Engage, Educate, Elevate

- **Identify and Engage with Difficult Individuals:**
  - Recognize challenging personalities and situations in your work environment.
  - Approach difficult interactions with a mindset of learning and growth.
  - Initiate conversations with individuals you find challenging to understand their perspectives.

- **Understanding the Value of Difficult Situations:**
  - Acknowledge that difficult situations teach resilience, patience, and critical thinking.
  - Appreciate the lessons learned from overcoming adversity and navigating complex scenarios.
  - Embrace the growth opportunities that come from dealing with difficult people and situations.

- **Maximizing Your Growth from Difficult Experiences:**
  - Reflect on each challenging encounter and identify the skills you developed.
  - Implement the lessons learned to improve your professional and personal interactions.
  - Share your experiences and the growth you've achieved with peers and mentors, demonstrating your resilience and adaptability.

> My goal with Chapter 7 is to emphasize the significance of navigating difficult people and challenging situations in shaping your personal and professional development. By sharing my experiences and the lessons I learned, I aim to provide you with the tools to engage with challenging individuals, understand the value of difficult situations, and maximize your growth from these experiences. This chapter underscores the importance of resilience, integrity, and critical thinking in overcoming obstacles and achieving success. In the next chapter, we will highlight the differences between pre-apprenticeships and apprenticeships.

With Baltimore City students in 2023 at the Operating Engineers Training Center in Baltimore County, using virtual simulation machines. (Credit: Corrin Johnson)

CHAPTER 8:

Pre-Apprenticeships Versus Apprenticeships

I remember the day Rik asked me if I wanted to make some extra money. It was on Edgewood Street in Edmondson Village, a narrow road concentrated with row homes, where drugs flowed from one block and the next. I was 14, with a hustler's instinct, but something inside me trembled knowing that the offer was wrong.

In the seventh and eighth grades, I had been approached by older teenagers in the neighborhood. I thought they were cool, but I never saw myself as a drug dealer. I had hopes of being "successful," even if I didn't know what that meant. I rejected the offers, but high school brought new challenges, and I needed cash. My mother was too busy trying to meet expenses while working two jobs, and I didn't want to burden her with a request she couldn't fulfill.

In middle school, I peddled bubble gum, snacks, and beedi—small cigarettes I sold for 25 cents each to classmates to keep money in my pocket. Most jobs in Baltimore City required you to be sixteen, and I had lost my job delivering *The Baltimore Sun* newspaper in my neighborhood after moving to my grandmother's house for the second time.

Rik was a couple of years older than me. With his offer, the stakes grew higher.

He said if I sold 10 dime bags of weed, I could keep $30 while he got $70. The math seemed simple, but I felt pangs of fear mixed with excitement. I was about to make some money, but the danger level shot up ten notches.

Over the past several years of living on Edgewood Street, I considered teenagers older than me like cousins; not just Rik, but Lucky, Phats, and others. I knew they had my back, but I would learn the hard way that crossing them was dangerous.

I sold those ten bags quickly at school. It was easy, too easy. I knew all the people who smoked weed before school. I sold to them in the morning at the local gas station, and during the day around lunchtime. I got a package from Rik four or five more times, but the unease lingered.

Then my mind, always scheming for a better way, found a gap. I asked an older friend how much an ounce of weed cost and if he would sell me one. The price was between $60 and $70. If I made 12 dime bags from an ounce, I calculated, I could make up to $60 instead of Rik's $30. I felt a thrill, thinking I had outsmarted the game. I was ready to take the next steps, unaware of the unseen costs.

I bought my first ounce from one of the older boys in my grandmother's neighborhood. There it was, a plastic sandwich bag of green buds with a potent aroma. I remember the mix of pride and nerves as I walked into the corner store at the intersection of Harford Road and Carswell Street to buy more bags to package the weed. At my mother's home, I closed my bedroom door and fumbled with the buds, trying to eyeball the right amount for each package. My heart pounded. I was unsure if I was measuring it right.

Business was booming until Rik realized I had cut him out. I was selling 80 percent of my marijuana at school and the rest on Edgewood Street. Rik seemed nonchalant, but he was hiding his anger. He was playing chess while I played checkers.

One day, two of his boys cornered me and took several bags of the weed I was selling. Rik had set me up, without warning.

I was shocked and unprepared. I knew how to defend myself from my time at Boys' Village, but this was a different level of threat.

I called my brother, frantic and upset. Within an hour, my brother, my sister, and a cousin arrived, ready to make those who had robbed me pay.

We went to the basketball court at the Mary E. Rodman school and recreation center, where everyone hung out if they weren't on Edgewood Street. We interrupted the game and my brother asked, "Who was it?"

I pointed out one of the boys, named Box. My brother grabbed him by the hair and started throwing punches. My heart pounded as we fought at least five people in the middle of the basketball court, with spectators watching. The adrenaline masked my fear, but I knew this wasn't a game anymore. Here we were, one action triggering another.

As we walked back to my sister's car, Lil Jon, the second boy who had taken my weed, followed behind. Our cousin pulled out a gun, its cold metal a reminder of the dangerous reality enveloping us. The weapon sent a message: We were not to be messed with. I'll never forget the stillness and fear I saw in Lil Jon's eyes.

As Lil Jon stood frozen, my brother floored him with one punch. We rode off, but the fear—and resolve—stayed with me.

I paid no heed to the signs that told me to walk away from the drug business. Within months, I was going harder. Ounces turned into pounds, I built a small business, and I had people working for me on the same 70-30 split. The lessons from my encounter with Rik should have pushed me away from the drug trade, but instead they drove me closer to it.

Pre-Apprenticeship: The Right Path for Some

The ways that people get into and out of the drug game are different for everyone. Similarly, the doors to apprenticeships can be different.

I was lucky to have a mother who pushed me to apply. Others have family members or neighbors with knowledge.

Some people start on the path toward becoming an apprentice by entering programs known as pre-apprenticeships. In my experience, these programs come with major risks and downsides, but they do serve a purpose for the right candidates.

Pre-apprenticeships are best suited for those who need help with soft skills such as showing up to work on time and functioning in professional settings, along with basic math and writing.

A pre-apprenticeship program need not take more than six to twelve weeks.

However, some students may be lured in by for-profit programs lasting twelve to eighteen months, and offering no real advantage to someone applying to an apprenticeship for the first time. Those who are lured by the marketing practices of some of these for-profit programs lose one of the most important assets they have in life: their time.

If a pre-apprenticeship program offers guaranteed access to employment or an apprenticeship after completion, it may be worthwhile. But for those spending six to eight hours in a classroom without real guarantees, the value is dubious.

Many for-profit pre-apprenticeship programs—and some nonprofit programs—target minority communities already plagued with disinvestment. Many enrollees are just coming home from incarceration or graduating from high school without a clear blueprint for what's next, working odd jobs and looking for a better career path. These young people and those trying to help them—like guidance and career counselors—must arm themselves with knowledge to make sure the pre-apprenticeship program is right for them.

Most pre-apprenticeships are focused on classroom instruction, without an on-the-job training component that is so important to success. If a young person has a high school degree with a solid GPA, they can save time and gain direct access to many construction and building trades without more classroom time.

I have witnessed friends graduating from their pre-apprenticeship programs, only to be told to directly apply to the IBEW apprenticeship program. This frustrates me, because they wasted time. I hope this book saves future apprentices time and money on their career journeys.

Unfortunately, a significant amount of local, state, and federal grant resources go to nonprofits for career training, with little accountability and a lack of partnerships that could have provided direct access to employment after completion of a pre-apprenticeship program.

I don't blame the instincts of elected officials from both parties who support career training. But many officeholders do not fully understand how apprenticeships work, and may be compounding our problems by directing resources to programs that communicate hope but fail to deliver results.

If you are looking for a credible pre-apprenticeship program, here are questions to ask:
- How long is the pre-apprenticeship program?
- How much does it cost?
- What skills will be learned?
- Are there opportunities for hands-on experiences or internships?
- Can they list their employer partnerships?
- Do they have direct access to employment after completion?
- What is the success rate of participants in securing apprenticeships or employment?

- Does the program offer certification or credentials recognized by employers in the industry?
- What support services are provided, such as wraparound services, job placement, and financial aid or scholarships?
- How does the program help develop essential soft skills like communication, teamwork, and problem-solving?
- Are there alumni success stories?
- What follow-up support or mentorship is available?

Parents and guidance counselors should review these questions so they can help students make informed decisions.

As discussed previously, apprenticeship programs are regulated and registered by labor departments, while pre-apprenticeship programs may not be. State and federal labor departments can help settle grievances if contractual obligations of an apprenticeship aren't met. This isn't the case for pre-apprenticeships, which may not have rigorous guidelines.

I have spoken to classes and at graduation ceremonies of pre-apprenticeship programs. I have seen the happy faces of the parents as their children move toward employment. Connections with an employer or apprenticeship program should take place within days of completion of a pre-apprenticeship program if is truly in the business of providing life-changing experiences.

If you are a student who has participated in a for-profit pre-apprenticeship program, please return to Chapter 2 and review the advice to immediately "move to action." Hopefully this book has provided a path forward and increased your chances of getting accepted into an apprenticeship.

The Power of Informed Decisions

As I reflect on my journey from the streets to a structured apprenticeship, I recognize the value of informed decisions. Knowledge and guidance can transform lives. Whether you're a young adult considering career options, a parent eager to support your child's future, or a guidance counselor committed to providing the best advice, understanding the landscape of apprenticeships and pre-apprenticeships is crucial.

Apprenticeships offer a pathway to a fulfilling career, with hands-on training, mentorship, and the opportunity to earn while you learn. They are rigorous and regulated, ensuring that every apprentice receives quality education and practical experience. In contrast, pre-apprenticeships can be a stepping stone for those who need to build foundational skills but should be chosen carefully to avoid programs that waste time and resources.

To all the young people out there, remember that your hustle and determination can lead to success, but it's the informed choices that will sustain it. Seek out credible programs, ask the right questions, and don't be afraid to demand the best for your future. Your journey is unique, and with the right support, you can build a career that not only provides stability but also brings pride and purpose.

To parents and guidance counselors, your role is pivotal. By staying informed and involved, you can help guide the next generation toward opportunities that will set them on a path to success. Engage in conversations about apprenticeships, explore the options available, and ensure that the young adults in your life have access to the information they need to make empowered decisions.

Together, we can build a future where every young person has the tools and opportunities to thrive. Let's break the cycle of misinformation and unlock the potential within our communities, one informed decision at a time.

Life Lessons Through Apprenticeships

Engage, Educate, Elevate

- **Understanding Pre-Apprenticeships:**
  - Recognize Their Role: Pre-apprenticeships are designed to help you build foundational skills such as punctuality, basic writing and math, and workplace etiquette.
  - Who They're For: Pre-apprenticeships are best suited for those of you who need to develop essential soft skills. If you feel unprepared for a professional setting, a pre-apprenticeship can be a great start.
  - Evaluate Programs: When looking at pre-apprenticeship programs, consider their length, their cost, and the specific skills they promise to teach. Make sure they align with your personal needs and career goals.

- **Navigating Apprenticeships:**
  - Understand the Structure: Apprenticeships are regulated programs that offer hands-on training, mentorship, and a clear path to a rewarding career.
  - Direct Entry: Many of you can enter apprenticeships directly if you already possess the necessary skills and knowledge. Don't feel obligated to go through a pre-apprenticeship if you are ready for the next step.
  - Benefits: Apprenticeships allow you to earn while you learn, combining practical experience with quality education. This dual approach ensures you gain valuable skills and financial stability.

- **Asking the Right Questions:**

- » Duration and Cost: How long is the pre-apprenticeship program, and what will it cost you?
- » Skills and Experience: What specific skills will you learn, and are there opportunities for hands-on experience or internships?
- » Employer Connections: Does the program have strong partnerships with employers, and will it provide direct access to job opportunities after completion?
- » Success Rates: What is the success rate of participants in securing apprenticeships or employment?
- » Credentials: Will you earn certifications or credentials that are recognized by employers in the industry?
- » Support Services: What support services are available, such as job placement assistance, financial aid, and wraparound services?
- » Soft Skills Development: How does the program help you develop essential soft skills like communication, teamwork, and problem-solving?
- » Alumni Success: Are there any success stories from past participants, and does the program offer follow-up support or mentorship?

- **Making Informed Decisions:**
  - » Importance of Information: Making informed choices is crucial. Understand the differences between pre-apprenticeships and apprenticeships, and choose the path that best suits your needs.
  - » Seek Guidance: Don't hesitate to ask for advice from your parents, guidance counselors, and mentors. They can provide valuable insights and help you explore the best career pathways.
  - » Explore Options: Engage in conversations about apprenticeships, investigate various programs, and ensure you make empowered and informed decisions about your future.

- **Empowering Future Apprentices:**
  - » Leverage Your Drive: Your hustle and determination can lead to success, but informed choices will help sustain it. Seek out credible programs, ask the right questions, and don't be afraid to demand the best for your future.
  - » Support Systems: Parents and guidance counselors play a pivotal role in your journey. By staying informed and involved, they can help guide you toward opportunities that foster growth and stability.
  - » Community Empowerment: Together, we can break the cycle of misinformation and unlock the potential within every young person, ensuring that you have the tools and opportunities to thrive.

> My goal with Chapter 8 is to highlight the differences between pre-apprenticeships and apprenticeships, emphasizing the importance of making informed decisions when choosing a career path. By sharing my experiences, I aim to provide you with the knowledge to recognize the value of each program and make choices that align with your goals. In the next chapter, we will explore a variety of trades and apprenticeship programs, including those in growing fields like health care and tech, to help you find the ideal path for your future.

Standing in front of the Carpenters Training Center in Baltimore with CollegeBound students during one of our many apprenticeship tours.

CHAPTER 9:

Understanding the Different Trade Apprenticeships

I stood on a stage at age twenty-five, my heart pounding with fear, yet feeling an unshakable determination to share my story.

I was only a few months from my IBEW apprenticeship graduation and had been invited to speak at an event called "Alternative Pathways Forward," hosted by Rep. Elijah Cummings, our beloved 7th District congressman, at Coppin State University.

As I scanned the room filled with over a hundred students and parents, all faces of color, I saw myself in their eyes. They were searching for a way out, a path forward, an escape from life's harsh realities. The hope in the parents' faces was palpable; they were desperately seeking something positive for their young scholars, and someone they could relate to and draw inspiration from.

Congressman Cummings, a master orator, approached the podium, glanced at his notes, then set them aside, opting to speak from the heart. He recounted his humble beginnings as the son of a sharecropper, and explained why we were gathered together on this Saturday morning. He spoke of the community's struggles, the purpose of the event, and the opportunities he aimed to provide for those who were often overlooked. His words resonated deeply as he described how he helped find jobs for the young men outside his home on Madison Avenue, emphasizing our collective responsibility.

He waved his hands as he moved across the stage, his voice rising and falling with passion. Congressman Cummings conveyed the weight of systemic frustrations and stressed the responsibility we all bear when opportunities present themselves. Then he called me up to the front of the room.

The white tie around my neck felt foreign and constricting and I nervously began to tell my story—my real story. I spoke of a broken juvenile justice system and the youth trapped within it, of L Section in the city jail, of a criminal justice system that created more broken young people than it rehabilitated.

I shared the story of a young man who had turned eighteen in Baltimore City Jail and had given up hope, and of a mother who never gave up on her son, guiding him toward an apprenticeship that changed his life.

As I spoke, the room fell silent. Parents and their children seemed to hang on each word. There were moments when I paused, remembering how the streets had taught me to move in silence and stay under the radar. But an inner voice urged me on: "Cory, you've crossed the finish line, and others are trying to follow."

I saw my mother's proud face in the crowd, witnessing her son's transformation from his lowest point to his best self. My mentors, Dave Norfolk and Rod Easter, were there too, proud witnesses to my journey.

When I finished my remarks and sat down, Congressman Cummings summoned me back to the podium. "This one of the most touching speeches I have ever heard," he said, adding that he knew I had reached the audience "because of how old you are and what you've been through." He gave me a hug, and in that moment, my pathway to public service cracked open.

Young scholars from local high schools and the Job Corps program in Woodstock, Maryland, approached me afterward with handshakes and the embrace we call the Baltimore salute, expressing respect and a desire to stay connected, seeking guidance on their own paths.

From that day forward, I made it a point to participate in Congressman Cummings' "Alternative Pathways Forward" event every year, continuing to share my story in hopes of inspiring others. That day marked a turning point in my life, eventually leading me to elected office in Maryland.

As the years passed, I noticed subtle changes in the audience. Faces grew more hopeful, the questions more insightful. I would often linger after my speeches, talking with the young men and women who were eager to carve out their own paths, much as I had. Their stories were varied but contained the same themes of struggle and resilience. They spoke of obstacles that seemed insurmountable, of dreams deferred, and of the hopes that kept them moving forward.

I recall one young man in particular, Jamal, who approached me after one of my speeches. He was on the brink of dropping out of high school, feeling burdened by life. We talked at length about his aspirations and the hurdles he faced. I connected him with an apprenticeship program, much like the one that had saved me. A year later, Jamal returned to the event, full of pride and determination, having found his way in the world.

These moments reinforced my belief in the power of sharing our stories. The connections forged in those brief interactions often blossomed into mentorships and lifelong friendships. Each narrative shared was a thread in the fabric of our community, binding us together in our pursuit of better futures.

My journey from that first speech to my role as a state senator was fueled by these interactions. They kept me grounded and reminded me of the importance of representation and accessibility. The lessons I learned from Congressman Cummings, his dedication to service, and his unwavering belief in the potential of every individual, continued to guide my path.

While I have been proud of my career as a union electrician, the "alternative pathways" championed by Congressman Cummings include many different trades, with their own strengths and appeals.

We will explore them in the remainder of this chapter, in a way that may inspire young people to recognize their value.

1. Carpenters

Carpenters are the backbone of construction, artisans who transform blueprints into tangible structures. These skilled craftworkers start by setting the frames for concrete that are the foundations of buildings, ensuring stability from the ground up. They build walls using wood or metal studs, constructing the framework that will support the rest of the structure. With precision, they hang drywall, install windows and doors, and fit cabinets and other fixtures. Details matter, from the correct placement of a door to the trim work that gives a room its finished look. Carpenters shape the spaces where we live, work, and play, turning architects' visions into reality with their hands and tools.

2. Cement Masons

Cement masons are the craftsmen who shape our built environment with their expertise in concrete. They pour, level, and finish concrete to create smooth, durable surfaces for foundations, floors, sidewalks, and more. Their skill ensures that each surface not only looks flawless but also stands the test of time. Cement masons are also responsible for the repair and maintenance of existing concrete structures, addressing cracks and wear to preserve safety and longevity. Their mastery of various concrete mixtures and finishing techniques is vital in both new construction and renovation projects.

3. Electricians

Electricians are the vital hands behind the power systems that illuminate our lives. They install and maintain electrical systems in homes, commercial buildings and industrial facilities. Electricians ensure that we have reliable power for lighting, heating, and appliances, creating the backbone of modern convenience. Following blueprints, they plan the layout of electrical systems, meticulously installing wiring, outlets, and circuit breakers. When issues arise, electricians troubleshoot and repair to keep systems running smoothly. Their work enables the technologies and comforts we often take for granted.

4. Elevator Constructors

Elevator constructors are the engineers of vertical mobility, ensuring that buildings are accessible and efficient. They install and maintain elevators, escalators, and moving walkways, integrating complex mechanical and electrical systems to provide smooth and safe transportation. With a growing emphasis on Americans with Disabilities Act compliance, their work is crucial in making buildings accessible to everyone. Elevator constructors must regularly update their knowledge of the latest technologies and safety standards to keep up with advancements in the industry. Their expertise ensures that we can move easily between floors in our homes, offices, and public spaces.

5. Ironworkers

Ironworkers are the pioneers of the construction site, the first to lay the skeletal framework of buildings and bridges. They fearlessly work at great heights, assembling steel beams with precision to ensure the structural integrity of the entire project. Their work provides the backbone that supports all other construction elements, from walls to roofs. Ironworkers must possess a deep understanding of structural engineering and the ability to work in challenging and often hazardous conditions.

6. Maintenance Workers

Maintenance workers are the unsung heroes of large facilities, ensuring that everything runs smoothly and efficiently. Employed to care for hospitals, schools, universities, and other significant buildings, they tackle a wide range of tasks—from electrical and plumbing repairs to HVAC maintenance and general upkeep. Their work ensures that these complex environments remain safe, functional, and comfortable for everyone. Through apprenticeships, aspiring maintenance workers receive hands-on training, preparing them for careers dedicated to the continuous improvement and operation of vital infrastructure. Building and construction crafts often cross over into maintenance work, where skilled individuals perform similar tasks to those in construction, but focus on the upkeep and functionality of large buildings.

7. Painters

Painters are the final artists in the construction process, bringing color and protection to houses, commercial buildings, or large infrastructure projects like bridges. The process begins with preparation—cleaning, sanding, and priming to create the perfect canvas. With an eye for detail and a steady hand, painters apply paint, stains, and coatings that enhance the aesthetic appeal and provide essential protection against the elements. Their work not only beautifies but also preserves, extending the lifespan of buildings and infrastructure through their skilled application of protective layers.

8. Plumbers and Steamfitters

Plumbers and steamfitters are the lifeline of modern infrastructure, ensuring the seamless flow of water, steam, and waste through a maze of pipes and valves. These experts install and maintain piping systems that provide clean water and efficient drainage in homes, offices, and public buildings. Steamfitters, a specialized branch, focus on systems that carry steam for heating and cooling applications, critical in industrial and large-scale commercial settings. They install and maintain refrigeration units for central air systems, keeping our environments comfortable and our groceries fresh. From the intricate plumbing in bathrooms and kitchens to the essential water heaters that provide our daily hot showers, their work ensures that our everyday lives run smoothly.

9. Roofers

Roofers shield our buildings from the forces of nature. These skilled professionals install, repair, and maintain roofs, working with materials such as shingles, metal, and rubber. Their expertise ensures that structures are protected from rain, wind, and sun, maintaining the integrity and longevity of our homes and commercial buildings. Understanding the nuances of different roofing systems, roofers apply techniques that guarantee durability and weather resistance. Their work is essential for maintaining the safety and functionality of our built environment.

10. Sheet Metal Workers

Sheet metal workers create the networks of ducts that breathe life into our buildings. Specializing in HVAC systems, they fabricate and install ductwork that ensures proper ventilation and climate control. Their expertise is critical to maintaining indoor air quality and the efficiency of HVAC systems in homes, schools, hospitals and more. Every bend and joint must be exact, because even the smallest error can erode the system's performance. Sheet metal workers play a vital role in creating comfortable, healthy environments for us to live and work in.

11. Welders

Welders use heat to join metal parts with precision and strength. Their work spans across various trades, from carpentry and electrical work to plumbing. Welding is crucial in constructing and repairing metal structures, whether it's the steel beams of a skyscraper, the pipelines that transport essential resources, or the machinery that drives industrial processes. Welders must master different techniques and materials, ensuring each bond is secure and durable.

Beyond Construction: Expanding Apprenticeships

Apprenticeships are growing beyond construction trades, into other fields such as health care, information technology (IT), and videography. This expansion reflects the evolving needs of our economy and the diverse opportunities available for hands-on training across various industries.

1. Health Care

Inside hospitals, young apprentices draw blood, prepare lab samples, or assist in patient care. These health care apprenticeships provide immersive experiences that blend theoretical knowledge with practical application. Participants become integral members of the health care team, learning medical procedures, patient interaction skills, and the importance of empathy in care. Programs may offer specializations in areas like phlebotomy, radiology, and medical coding. This comprehensive approach ensures that apprentices are well rounded, ready to tackle various challenges in future careers.

2. Information Technology

IT apprenticeships immerse participants in the world of technology, where they learn to navigate complex software, manage data, and protect digital infrastructures. These programs often include rotations through different departments, giving apprentices a holistic understanding of IT operations. They work on real projects, contributing to critical solutions while being mentored by industry experts. The result is a generation of tech professionals who are not only skilled but also adaptive, ready to lead in a constantly evolving digital landscape.

3. Videography

Videography apprenticeships offer a dynamic learning environment where creativity meets technical precision as students gain exposure to capturing scenes and directing lighting. Participants dive into every aspect of production, from storyboarding and scripting to shooting and post-production editing. They work closely with experienced filmmakers, gaining insights into the nuances of visual storytelling and the demands of the media industry. Apprentices emerge with portfolios showcasing their work, ready to pursue careers in film, television, advertising, or online content creation.

Adaptability and Relevance

The expansion of apprenticeships outside of trades illustrates the adaptability and relevance of this training model. By providing practical, hands-on experience and fostering industry-specific skills, apprenticeships create pathways to successful careers in many fields.

This approach benefits the apprentices themselves and also addresses critical workforce needs, ensuring that industries have the skilled professionals they require to thrive. As we continue to embrace and develop these programs, we unlock new opportunities for individuals to learn, grow, and contribute meaningfully to our society.

Every state is different, and it is incumbent upon those seeking opportunities to engage with their respective Department of Labor and immerse themselves in information about registered apprenticeships and their oversight. Understanding the landscape of these programs—both traditional and emerging—is a crucial first step.

Begin by researching the specific requirements and opportunities available in your state. Each Department of Labor office offers resources and guidance tailored to regional industries and workforce needs. Take the time to explore their websites, attend informational sessions, and reach out to apprenticeship coordinators for detailed insights.

Once you have a grasp of the options, apply research tips from previous chapters to develop a strategic plan. Identify the industries that align with your interests and career goals, and delve into the specifics of the apprenticeship programs within those fields. Understand the skills you will acquire, the duration of the training, and the potential for future employment. Look for programs that offer robust support systems, such as mentorship opportunities, hands-on training, and clear progression paths.

Networking is also a key component of your journey. Connect with current and former apprentices to gain first-hand perspectives on their experiences. Attend industry events, job fairs, and community workshops to meet professionals who can offer advice and potentially open doors for you. Building a network of contacts within your chosen field can provide invaluable support and guidance as you navigate your apprenticeship journey.

Additionally, consider the financial aspects of apprenticeships. Many programs offer stipends or wages that can help support you while you learn. Investigate scholarships, grants, and financial aid options that may be available to apprentices in your state. Balancing your financial needs with your educational and career goals is essential for long-term success.

Immerse yourself in continuous learning. Apprenticeships are just the beginning of your career journey. Stay updated with industry trends, new technologies, and evolving best practices. Participate in additional training, certifications, and educational opportunities to enhance your skills and stay competitive in the job market.

Remember, apprenticeships are more than just training programs—they are gateways to rewarding careers.

Embrace this journey with enthusiasm and determination. The opportunities are vast and varied, and with the right approach, you can carve a path that leads to a fulfilling and prosperous career. The skills you acquire, the connections you make, and the experiences you gain will equip you to face challenges, seize opportunities, and achieve your aspirations.

Life Lessons Through Apprenticeships

Engage, Educate, Elevate

- Engaging with Trades and Emerging Fields
  - » **Explore Various Roles:** Dive into the vital contributions of trades such as carpentry, plumbing, roofing, and electrical work. Each craft is essential in building and maintaining our infrastructure.
  - » **Hands-On Experience:** Seek out workshops or volunteer opportunities to get practical exposure to different trades and emerging fields like health care, IT, and videography.
  - » **Networking Opportunities:** Connect with industry professionals and mentors at events, job fairs, and community workshops to gain valuable insights and build relationships.

- Educating Yourself on Apprenticeships
  - » **Program Evaluation:** Research and assess apprenticeship programs by considering their length, cost, and the specific skills they teach. Make sure they align with your career aspirations.
  - » **Financial Planning:** Understand the financial aspects of apprenticeships, including stipends, wages, scholarships, and financial aid options available in your state.
  - » **Skill Development:** Focus on acquiring practical, hands-on experience in your chosen field. Look for programs that offer comprehensive support systems and mentorship opportunities.

- Making Informed Decisions
  - » **Engage with Resources:** Use your state's Department of Labor for detailed information on registered apprenticeship programs. Attend informational sessions and reach out to apprenticeship coordinators.
  - » **Seek Guidance:** Consult with parents, guidance counselors, and mentors for advice. They can provide valuable insights and help you explore the best career pathways.
  - » **Explore Options:** Investigate various apprenticeship programs and have informed discussions to ensure you make empowered decisions about your future.

> My goal with Chapter 9 is to illustrate the power of storytelling to highlight the value and impact of apprenticeship programs. By sharing my journey and experiences, I aim to articulate the importance of traditional apprenticeship crafts in the construction industry while also discussing the emerging opportunities in fields like health care, IT, and videography. This chapter seeks to provide you with a comprehensive understanding of both established and new apprenticeship pathways, helping you to see the vast possibilities available and guiding you to find the ideal path for your future.

An interview with the late Tim Tooten of WBAL-TV about the importance of apprenticeship pathways. (Credit: Corrin Johnson)

CHAPTER 10:

Apprentice to Entrepreneur

My decision to join the apprenticeship program was a turning point, a step into a world beyond my neighborhood.

On jobsites and in the union hall, I found myself in conversations with people who spoke passionately about owning homes, fixing things around the house, and running their own businesses. These discussions made me realize that my dreams could be far bigger.

Growing up, homeownership was not drilled into me as important. Most of my family members were renters. Owning a home seemed unattainable. But as I spent more time with people who valued homeownership, I realized the profound impact it could have on my life.

One day I made a call to a real estate office, and a seasoned agent, Michael Gallagher, picked up the phone. In a reassuring voice that conveyed honesty and eagerness to help, he explained the steps needed for homeownership—including getting preapproval for a mortgage.

As an apprentice, I was a member of the Electricians Union, which had a partnership with a credit union that could facilitate that preapproval. With the help of Michael and a banker, I secured a $65,000 Federal Housing Administration (FHA) loan, which would cover 100 percent of the purchase price of a home. I would only have to pay $3,500 in closing costs for my first home, at age twenty.

For a few weeks on Sundays, Michael and I drove around, looking at homes across the city, seeking the best price and the right fit.

We found a property on Woodlea Avenue in the Gardenville neighborhood, adjacent to Belair-Edison in Northeast Baltimore City. It was a modest three-bedroom house with a garage and a half-finished basement. My mortgage would be less than $600 a month—a manageable amount for someone working up to 70 hours a week in my apprenticeship and at my part-time Home Depot job.

Carrying the responsibility of a mortgage at such a young age was daunting. I was balancing work, the apprenticeship and classes, and needed to close on the property in sixty days. But I still took the plunge, knowing it was the right step.

In my second year of my apprenticeship, when I received a raise, I decided to invest in another property. The bug had been planted in me, I wanted to be an entrepreneur. I diligently saved every extra dollar and began looking exclusively in the Belair-Edison neighborhood, an area I was familiar with and that I could afford.

I chose to use only about half of my preapproved amount for a second property, to maintain a manageable debt-to-income ratio. I found a house on Pelham Avenue, a two-bedroom property with central air conditioning and a parking pad, needing just a few cosmetic updates. It was a sound investment. If I had a $500 monthly mortgage, I could rent the property for $700 and make a profit.

After this second purchase, I began studying concepts like property value appreciation and tax reduction strategies so that I could apply what I was learning to future investments.

I now had a blueprint for success. I had a plan and stuck to it, while always looking for ways to improve. Fear often crept in, but I faced it, growing personally and professionally.

In the third year of my apprenticeship, I purchased a three-bedroom corner row home on Kenyon Avenue with a nice yard and porch. Like Pelham Avenue, Kenyon needed only cosmetic work. When a fire destroyed the kitchen in 2008, I did most of the repair work myself, learning the benefits of homeowners' insurance plus building my construction skills.

The following year, I took on a special project, a three-bedroom town home on Ravenwood Avenue. This property needed a lot of work, and I handled most of the renovations myself. I did the framing, drywall hanging, plumbing, tile work, electrical work and painting, and I installed an outside fence. The only tasks I didn't handle were the roof installation, the central air-conditioning unit, and the carpeting. I learned a lot about the value of hard work and the satisfaction of seeing a project through to completion.

In my fifth year, I bought two more homes: a two-bedroom row home on Chesterfield Avenue and a multiunit property on Biddison Avenue in the Frankford neighborhood, previously owned by the brother of former Baltimore Mayor Thomas D'Alesandro Jr. Like Pelham and Kenyon, Chesterfield and Biddison needed mostly cosmetic work, but each investment was carefully chosen for its potential.

By the age of twenty-five, I controlled properties worth more than $1 million and was ready to use my experience to guide others.

I was now effectively running a small real estate business. I developed several rules for myself.

I maintained relationships with several banks and a credit union, always shopping for the best interest rates. I preferred a fixed-rate mortgage over a variable rate to ensure stable and predictable payments.

While I had lines of credit, I used them solely for purchasing homes and always repaid the money promptly. This disciplined approach allowed me to maintain financial stability and avoid unnecessary debt.

As a landlord, I needed to develop rental applications and leases. I used my mentors' guidance and supplemented it with other information to create the best documents.

I paid my contractors fairly, and they were ready to help when needed. Building a sound contractor base that responds quickly to emergencies keeps tenants happy. I have always preferred contractors from the local community so I could reinvest in my neighborhood.

Every month, I would personally collect rent so that I could check on the home and tenants could see that I cared. This approach helped maintain the properties and build trust with the tenants. In fact, I only bought properties that I would live in myself.

In my own way, I was providing affordable housing by charging rent about 15 percent to 20 percent below the market rate, prices that drew a larger applicant pool. I try to limit rent increases, but sometimes pass along property tax and insurance rate hikes or higher maintenance costs.

Advertising for tenants became free when classified ads shifted to online. I had dozens of applicants for each property, and was proud to host open houses so prospective tenants could see the beautiful conditions.

For several years, I served on the Belair-Edison Community Board because I believed in giving back to the neighborhood that was helping me accumulate wealth. I was vested in the sustainability of the neighborhood, its cleanliness, and public safety.

The journey wasn't always smooth. In 2011, the economy was tough, and I faced high vacancies. I realized I was leveraged pretty high and focused on paying down debt. This period taught me the importance of financial stability and prudent investment. Despite the challenges, I made more money than I lost. Every experience offered opportunities to grow: Negotiating with contractors, understanding the value of time, purchasing at the right price, and knowing when to walk away from a bad deal were lessons that can't be taken from me.

I also learned the importance of keeping good documents and records to ensure I was watching cash flow closely and taking responsibility for all local and state registrations. Ignorance is never an excuse.

I enjoy providing guidance to friends and young people about the benefits of real estate. I'm happy to share insights on negotiations and contracts, and on inspectors and contractors. It's one way to help build a community.

Throughout my journey, I have always immersed myself in books about successful entrepreneurs. I've been inspired by the stories of Reginald F. Lewis, Don Peebles, Herman J. Russell, A. G. Gaston, and Maggie L. Walker. Their experiences taught me about overcoming adversity, the importance of persistence, and the power of self-belief. Reading about great leaders was invaluable, especially when I lacked direct mentorship.

Reginald F. Lewis was one of the first African Americans to build a billion-dollar company. His story of overcoming racial barriers and achieving extraordinary success inspired me to push through my own challenges. Don Peebles' journey from a real estate broker to one of the wealthiest African American real estate developers taught me the value of resilience and strategic thinking.

Herman J. Russell's legacy as a construction and real estate mogul, despite the segregation and discrimination he faced, highlighted the power of vision and persistence. A. G. Gaston's rise from humble beginnings to creating a business empire showed me the importance of community and giving back. Maggie L. Walker, the first African American woman to charter a bank, exemplified leadership and innovation, proving that even the most formidable barriers could be overcome with determination and ingenuity.

Their achievements became benchmarks for what was possible, encouraging me to set higher goals and work tirelessly to achieve them.

To all aspiring apprentices and their parents, I advocate for homeownership as a crucial part of your legacy. Live within your means and ensure your mortgage is sustainable. With each property I acquired, I asked myself: Could I maintain this home if I were laid off or faced unforeseen challenges? This cautious yet ambitious approach has guided my decision-making.

The journey from an apprentice to an entrepreneur wasn't easy, but it was incredibly rewarding. Every challenge taught me a lesson, and every success reinforced my belief in the power of hard work, determination, and strategic thinking. As you embark on your own journeys, remember that your dreams are within reach. All it takes is the right mindset, a bit of guidance, and the willingness to seize every opportunity.

While I may have made money as an entrepreneur, the real fulfillment came in the wealth of experience I garnered. You can learn a lot from things you don't know and from being challenged to come up with solutions. This journey has been about more than just financial gain; it's been about personal growth, resilience, and the satisfaction of overcoming obstacles.

Life Lessons Through Apprenticeships

Engage, Educate, Elevate

- Engaging with Real Estate and Financial Management
  - » **Discover the Value of Real Estate:** Learn how owning property can be a crucial step toward financial independence. Understand the impact of homeownership on building wealth and stability for your future.
  - » **Hands-On Learning:** Seek opportunities to volunteer with housing projects, assist in home renovations, or shadow professionals in the real estate industry. Real-world experience is invaluable in understanding the dynamics of property investment.
  - » **Build a Network:** Connect with industry professionals, attend community workshops, job fairs, and networking events. Building relationships with mentors and professionals in the real estate and financial sectors can provide guidance and open doors to future opportunities. Parents can support their children by encouraging and facilitating these connections.

- Educating Yourself on Homeownership and Financial Literacy
  - » **Understanding Loans and Mortgages:** Learn about different types of loans (FHA, conventional) and the importance of getting preapproved. Understand how maintaining a good debt-to-income ratio can impact your financial health.
  - » **Financial Planning:** Gain insights into the financial aspects of purchasing and maintaining property, including closing costs and mortgages. Learn the importance of saving diligently and living within your means. Parents can help by discussing financial planning and budgeting with their children.

- » **Skill Development:** Focus on acquiring practical skills in property management, basic home repairs, and renovations. Look for programs that offer hands-on experience and mentorship in these areas. Both high schoolers and parents can explore these programs together to ensure they align with career goals.

- Making Informed Decisions
  - » **Use Resources:** Use local resources such as credit unions, real estate agencies, and financial consultants for detailed information on homebuying and property management.
  - » **Seek Guidance:** Consult with mentors, real estate professionals, and financial advisers. Their insights can help you navigate the complexities of property investment and homeownership. Parents can provide support by helping their children find and connect with these mentors.
  - » **Explore Options:** Research various real estate investment strategies and property management practices. Make informed decisions about building your real estate portfolio to secure your financial future.

By understanding the principles of real estate investment and financial management, high schoolers and their parents can build a strong foundation for a stable and prosperous future. Engage with the right resources, educate yourself continuously, and make informed decisions to achieve your goals. Parents can play a crucial role in guiding and supporting their children through this journey, ensuring they have the knowledge and tools needed to succeed.

My goal with Chapter 10 is to demonstrate the transformative power of apprenticeships and financial literacy in achieving personal and financial independence. By sharing my journey from an apprentice to a property owner with a portfolio worth $1 million by the age of twenty-five, I aim to highlight the importance of homeownership and real estate investment as viable and rewarding career paths. This chapter seeks to provide high school students and their parents with a clear understanding of how apprenticeships can lead to significant financial opportunities, the value of practical, hands-on learning, and the crucial role of mentorship and networking. By the end of this chapter, I hope to inspire young individuals to explore real estate and financial management and equip them with the knowledge and confidence to embark on their own journeys toward financial stability and success.

Spending time in my newly assigned legislative office with my family before my 2019 swearing-in to the Maryland State Senate. (L to R: Demetria, Bryson, Cory, Cory Jr. (CJ), Reagan, Kennedy)

CHAPTER 11:
Additional Resources

Apprenticeships provide a structured pathway into skilled trades, offering hands-on experience, classroom instruction, and paid employment while learning. Whether you are looking to start a career, switch industries, or expand your expertise, these resources will help guide you toward available apprenticeship opportunities.

National Apprenticeship and Readiness Resources

U.S. Department of Labor – ApprenticeshipUSA: A comprehensive resource for apprenticeship programs across various industries, including construction, health care, manufacturing, and technology. A searchable database of registered apprenticeships, funding opportunities, and employer resources is available. (www.apprenticeship.gov)

North America's Building Trades Unions (NABTU): NABTU represents 14 national and international building trades unions, supporting pre-apprenticeship and apprenticeship programs that lead to well-paying careers. Includes programs that prepare individuals, particularly from underserved communities, for entry into building trades apprenticeships. (www.nabtu.org/apprenticeship-readiness-program)

Helmets to Hardhats: A national program that connects military service members and veterans with career training and employment opportunities in the construction industry through registered apprenticeships. (www.helmetstohardhats.org)

CareerOneStop (U.S. Department of Labor): A resource for finding apprenticeship opportunities, job training, and career planning. (www.careeronestop.org)

Apprenticeship Readiness Programs (NABTU): Prepare individuals, particularly from underserved communities, for entry into building trades apprenticeships. (www.nabtu.org)

Apprenticeship Programs for Women

Women in Apprenticeship and Nontraditional Occupations (WANTO) Grant Program: A U.S. Department of Labor initiative supporting women pursuing careers in skilled trades and nontraditional occupations through grants and training. (https://www.dol.gov/agencies/wb/grants/wanto)

National Center for Women's Equity in Apprenticeship and Employment: Hosted by Chicago Women in Trades, this center provides strategies and support to increase women's participation and retention in registered apprenticeships. (www.womensequitycenter.org)

Tradeswomen Inc.: Partners with programs to recruit women and enhance the capacity of pre-apprenticeship programs to train and place women in skilled trades. (www.tradeswomen.org)

Technology Apprenticeship Programs

Apprenti: A nationally recognized program providing paid apprenticeships in technology roles such as software development, cybersecurity, and network administration. Apprenti partners with companies to create career pathways for individuals from diverse backgrounds. (www.apprenticareers.org)

NPower: A national nonprofit offering free tech training for military veterans and young adults from underserved communities. Its Tech Fundamentals program includes in-class instruction and a paid internship to prepare individuals for entry-level tech roles. (www.npower.org)

Union-Based Apprenticeship Programs

International Brotherhood of Electrical Workers (IBEW): Offers high-quality electrical apprenticeship programs through the National Electrical Contractors Association (NECA) and Joint Apprenticeship and Training Committees (JATCs) nationwide. (www.ibew.org)

United Association of Plumbers and Pipefitters (UA): Provides five-year registered apprenticeships for careers in plumbing, pipefitting, HVAC, and welding. (https://ua.org/education-and-training/become-an-apprentice/)

International Union of Operating Engineers (IUOE): Operates training centers across the country for heavy equipment operators, mechanics, and stationary engineers. (www.iuoe.org/training)

International Association of Sheet Metal, Air, Rail, and Transportation Workers (SMART): Offers apprenticeship programs in sheet metal work, HVAC, welding, and transit through local training centers. (www.smart-union.org)

United Brotherhood of Carpenters and Joiners of America (UBC): Provides apprenticeships in carpentry, millwright work, and interior systems. (www.carpenters.org)

International Union of Elevator Constructors (IUEC): Offers apprenticeships for elevator installation, repair, and maintenance. (www.iuec.org)

United Union of Roofers, Waterproofers, & Allied Workers: Provides apprenticeships for roofing, waterproofing, and related building protection trades. (www.unionroofers.com)

International Union of Painters and Allied Trades (IUPAT): Trains apprentices in painting, drywall finishing, glazing, and sign work. (www.iupat.org)

Operative Plasterers' & Cement Masons' International Association (OPCMIA): Trains apprentices in plastering, cement masonry, and finishing. (www.opcmia.org)

International Union of Bricklayers and Allied Craftworkers (BAC): Provides apprenticeships in bricklaying, tile setting, and stonemasonry. (www.bacweb.org)

ACKNOWLEDGMENTS

This book is the result of faith, determination and the power of community. Every journey is shaped by the people who walk alongside us, and this one is no different.

The journey into uncharted territory comes with uncertainty, obstacles and moments of doubt. But the magic happens when you keep pushing, despite the "no's," until you reach the finish line. Every challenge became a stepping stone, and I wouldn't be here without those who walked beside me.

To my wife: Since we were 17 years old, you have been my rock, my greatest partner, and the person who has pushed me to be better in every way. We have faced every challenge together, hand in hand, and because of you, I stand stronger today. To my children: Thank you for grounding me, for reminding me of what truly matters, and for being the inspiration behind everything I do.

To my family: Your love and sacrifices shaped the man I am today. My mother, Renee McCray: You gave it your all, you poured everything into me and because of you, I am who I am. My grandmother, Sadie Foster: You gave everything to your grands and great-grands, always putting family first. My grandmother, Emily McCray: Your counsel and wisdom have guided me through the years, and I am forever grateful. My sister Danielle: You have always encouraged my dreams and never once discouraged my vision. My big brother Bernie: You poured into me the best way you knew how, and together we are the ones breaking cycles. My big sister Charmaine: you have always had my back, pushing for our success and making sure we stood tall.

To the people of Baltimore—whose grit, grind, hunger, and hustle continue to push me forward—this book is for you. My early years at Rognel Heights Elementary set the foundation for me outside of my home. In a tough city, my principal, Sarah Horsey, and my teachers, Ms. Lyde, Ms. Solomon, Ms. McCoy, Ms. Allen, and Ms. Linear, showed me love and guidance that I will always carry with me. Baltimore: Your stories, your struggles and your wins are the heart of my work. Every day, I am inspired by the resilience and brilliance of this city. We are not just building a better Baltimore; we are setting a standard for what's possible.

To the International Brotherhood of Electrical Workers and all my brothers and sisters in the trade, you have profoundly impacted my life and shifted my trajectory. To my classmate, my friend, my brother Jerome Miller: Thank you for always encouraging me and leading for our local union. Gary Griffin, thank you for taking a chance on me as I graduated as a journeyman in the IBEW. Though he is no longer with us, Ernie Grecco of the Baltimore Metropolitan Council AFL-CIO not only educated me on the importance of labor unions but also guided me through my first election. His mentorship and belief in me will never be forgotten. The lessons learned, the discipline instilled, and the opportunities created through the brotherhood of the IBEW and the leadership of labor giants like the Baltimore Metropolitan Council AFL-CIO have shaped me into the leader I am today.

To my thought partners: Michael Tubbs, our shared fellowship and your book, *The Deeper the Roots*, pushed me to expand my vision. Your leadership has inspired me to be bolder for Baltimore, and I'm grateful for the example you've set. Brian White and Matt Kayser, your relentless push for excellence in design and presentation set the bar, and this book cover is a testament to that standard. Sophia Silbergeld, thank you for being a thought partner on this project and helping bring it to life. Kevin Slayton, Kevin Shird, Chris Wilson, Ronald J. Daniels and Corrin Adams—thank you for offering guidance, encouragement and insight through your own journeys as published authors. Your examples helped me navigate this process with confidence and clarity.

To my mentors, colleagues and friends, your wisdom and encouragement refined my leadership, expanded my vision, and deepened my thinking. Theo Rodgers, Joseph Haskins, Keiffer Mitchell, Kurt Schmoke, Stu Simms, Clarence Mitchell IV, Carl Stokes, Ron Lipscomb, Michael R. Smith and Kweisi Mfume—strong Black male mentors who have poured into me during pivotal moments—your leadership, guidance, and example have shaped my path. Celinda Lake, your guidance and counsel over the years—especially in connecting me with Morgan James Publishing—have helped illuminate the path forward. To my sister Alicia Wilson, a daughter of Baltimore, your leadership inspires me to act with purpose and always reach for my North Star. To Morgan James Publishing, thank you for supporting me every step of the way and helping me navigate this process with clarity and confidence. Jermaine Jones, your presence and willingness to hear me out have meant the world. Your belief in my purpose has fueled me in ways words cannot capture.

Brandon Scott, my friend and brother, you have always been someone I could call on for advice and I am proud to see you representing our city to its fullest. You are our quarterback, leading for our generation.

To my childhood friend Anthony McKissett: While I didn't write in detail about many of our experiences, I carry them with me. We grew up together, learned life's hardest lessons side by side, and now strive to raise our children with more than we had. There are so many others who didn't get to cross that finish line, and we owe it to them to shift the trajectory for their sons and daughters still trying to figure it out.

A special thanks to my editor, David Nitkin, for his sharp eye and steady guidance in bringing this manuscript to completion.

To my team and everyone who helped bring this project to life, I thank you. The dedication, late nights, and commitment to excellence made this book one I am truly proud of.

And finally, to every reader who picks up this book: Thank you for investing your time, your energy, and your spirit into this journey. This book is not just a reflection of my path, it is a tribute to all those who believed in me, challenged me, and walked alongside me. Thank you for being part of this story. May these words challenge you to think bigger, move bolder and step into your purpose with intention.

ABOUT THE AUTHOR

Cory V. McCray is a union electrician, business owner, and policy champion who transformed his apprenticeship experience into a platform for change. Born and raised in Baltimore City, McCray navigated the challenges of the juvenile justice system before finding stability and purpose through the skilled trades. His journey from electrical apprentice to the Maryland State Senate is a testament to the power of opportunity, discipline, and perseverance. As the only member of the Maryland General Assembly to have completed an apprenticeship, McCray has dedicated his career to breaking down barriers and expanding pathways to success for working families.

A devoted husband and father of four, he is committed to ensuring that young people, regardless of background, have access to life-changing opportunities. In *The Apprenticeship That Saved My Life*, McCray blends personal narrative with practical guidance, offering a road map to success for the next generation of apprentices, entrepreneurs, and change-makers.

A free ebook edition is available with the purchase of this book.

To claim your free ebook edition:

1. Visit MorganJamesBOGO.com
2. Sign your name CLEARLY in the space
3. Complete the form and submit a photo of the entire copyright page
4. You or your friend can download the ebook to your preferred device

A **FREE** ebook edition is available for you or a friend with the purchase of this print book.

CLEARLY SIGN YOUR NAME ABOVE

Instructions to claim your free ebook edition:
1. Visit MorganJamesBOGO.com
2. Sign your name CLEARLY in the space above
3. Complete the form and submit a photo of this entire page
4. You or your friend can download the ebook to your preferred device

Print & Digital Together Forever.

Snap a photo   Free ebook   Read anywhere

www.ingramcontent.com/pod-product-compliance
Lightning Source LLC
Jackson TN
JSHW021911230825
89861JS00002B/3